Be Victorious

A 40-day devotional to help you defeat the enemy
the Jesus way, winning the battle with our ultimate
weapon: the Word of God

Helen Roberts

RIVER
PUBLISHING

River Publishing & Media Ltd
Bradbourne Stables
East Malling
Kent
ME19 6DZ
United Kingdom

info@river-publishing.co.uk

ISBN 978-1-908393-61-6
Cover design by www.spiffingcovers.com

Printed and bound by CPI Group (UK) Ltd, Croydon, CR0 4YY

CONTENTS

DEDICATION

To my absolute bestest friend on this planet! Hub, I love you completely. And to my three most favourites: Bethany, Hannah and David – I love you all. You are all the best parts of my day.

ACKNOWLEDGEMENTS

There are so many people who have helped make this book possible and I probably can't do justice to those who have prayed for me and encouraged me on this journey. So if you are one of them, thank you! But there are some that I simply must acknowledge by name.

Firstly, Tim – you are my best friend and co-worker for Christ. Without doubt, this book would not have happened without you. Thank you for encouraging me and championing me at every step. Thank you for loving me like you do.

To Bethany, Hannah and David – you all teach me so much about myself, about life, and about how to apply truth to be victorious. Thank you for helping me grow. May you be victorious in every situation you face because you are well-armed and living ready.

To all the Staff team and Senior Leadership team at Wellspring Church – thank you for encouraging me to respond to the Father's invitation for to me to write. Thank you for sharing the adventure and helping me find the space needed at various points along the way.

To Rebecca P – thank you for asking me questions. You ask great questions!

To Cathy D – thank you for your gifted eye for detail and your encouragement of the "rev boss lady".

To Jo N – thank you for the many chats over mugs of something, championing me, challenging me, refining me and encouraging me on to greater healing, freedom and victory.

To David O – thank you for being a spiritual father and mentor to me during those essential, foundational years of faith and inspiring me to love the Word of God more than I could have imagined.

To Tim Pettingale – thank you for catching my heart and believing in me. Thank you for being such an amazing "midwife" to this book-baby. And thank you to all the River team for seeing what I see in such a way that others can now see it too.

WHAT OTHERS ARE SAYING...

If you want to grow in your relationship with God and your knowledge of the Word, this beautifully written, easy-to-read devotional will help you on your journey. Rooted in Scripture and wonderfully practical, each day deals with a different, everyday issue to help you grow in God. Helen shares with refreshing honesty, real humility and lovely humour, making this book not only edifying, but also thoroughly enjoyable to read.
Pastor Jo Naughton, Church Leader, International speaker & author

More than a devotional, this small but mighty Bible study is practical, real, and a treasure-trove of wisdom and encouragement for the roller-coaster lives we so often live.
Abby Guinness, author and Spring Harvest Event Director

When we think of all that is ahead of us – we need strength. I love these devotions because they strengthen me. Take time and allow the Word of God, along with Helen's encouragements, to seep into your soul and do you good.
Mark Ritchie, Evangelist

This is a book each of us needs to read and then keep on a shelf for further use. Helen is a remarkable writer with an engaging style. Add to that her genuine honesty – describing the highs and lows of daily life in a way we can all relate to. But what makes *Be Victorious* most valuable is Helen's insightful use of Scripture. Verses you've probably read many times over will bring new light into your daily life, helping you live complete and victorious.

Joel Holm, Church/Missions Consultant, formerly of Willow Creek

Having known Helen now for a good number of years, this devotional testifies not just to her writing skills, but to how she lives life. *Be Victorious* will certainly help every reader to be the overcomer that the Bible teaches we are to be. I thoroughly recommend this excellent publication.

John Partington, National Leader AOG

Your next forty days never looked so good! Writing her debut devotional book, Helen ensures it is steeped in God's Word, rich with real life stories, and immensely practical in helping you win in every area of your life with Jesus. I can't commend this book highly enough.

Brian Somerville, Lead Pastor, Cornerstone City Church, Derry~Londonderry, N. Ireland

Helen brings to the grit and demands of everyday life, wisdom and insights you can live by; powerful truths from the Bible that she has experienced herself. She brings God's Word to life and I love the way she does that!

Debra Green OBE, Redeeming Our Communities

This wonderful book will sharpen faith, challenge complacency and renew vision by bringing to life the power of the Word of God for us in our everyday lives. Read it and become battle-ready, re-devoted soldiers in the army of God.
Dr Rachel Jordan-Wolf, National Adviser for Mission and Evangelism for the Church of England

Be Victorious so reflects Helen's own personality and journey that it abounds in authenticity, with touches of humour typical of its author. It is inspirational and accessible to read – a book to journey with and savour, not to skim through. Each day brings fresh and incisive insights into biblical truth and then applies that truth to real life. It is not a book for those who seek "quick fixes", but rather for those wanting true freedom through the process of a transformed mind and healed heart. Helen's vulnerability and disarming writing style enables us to face ourselves in the context of God's grace, love and healing. A great personal discipleship aid – transformational!
Peter & Mariette Stott, Church Consultants and Wellspring Church Apostolic Council

As I would expect from Helen, this book is honest, practical and describes how Scripture works where the rubber hits the road. By being honest about her own struggles and trials, as well as her triumphs and hilarious moments, the book draws us into the reality of life as she has lived it. Her own illustrations, together with lots of life scenarios from Scripture, make it an accessible, helpful and profitable way to take forty steps to increasing victory on forty consecutive days.
David Ollerton. Church leader and Chairman of Waleswide/ Cymrugyfan, a church-planting and strengthening network

At times life can be tough, but you can always find God in the middle of your struggle. Helen will help you to see Him regardless of what you are going through or facing. You will be encouraged and blessed by this devotional. Enjoy!

Ron Corzine, Christian Fellowship International, Fort Worth, Texas

FOREWORD

For as long as I can remember I've had a passionate love for the Word of God. It has given me a glimpse into the greatness and glory of the Lord, as well as providing me with wisdom, insight, guidance, direction and transformational truth. However, it's not just a holy book full of good ideas, but a God-breathed book that carries in its truth the very life of God. That's why I welcome and support any tool that helps people engage with the Word of God consistently and meaningfully, and I believe that *Be Victorious* is such a tool.

Proverbs tells us, *"He who gets wisdom loves his own soul; he who cherishes understanding prospers"* (Proverbs 19:8), and in this 40-day devotional we are being invited into the life-changing power of the Word of God. Each day represents a step on the journey deeper into His truth, where in the busyness of our world, we're encouraged to slow down, quieten our souls and tune in to ancient words that still speak profoundly into our 21st Century reality.

Be Victorious comes to you from the hand and heart of my friend Helen Roberts. Helen is a leader, wife, mother and teacher, as well as being one of the most authentic people I know. The chapters before you are not the product of spin and hype, but of spiritual substance, worked out in the crucible of her life, family, local church and community. I wholeheartedly recommend this book to you not only because of the Word-based wisdom it contains, but also because it comes from a Word-loving practioner.

Someone once said, "When we pray we talk to God, but when we read the Bible, God talks to us." May His Word dwell in your heart richly so that through His Word, the ultimate weapon, you will *Be Victorious!*

Dr John Andrews
Principal, Mattersey Hall

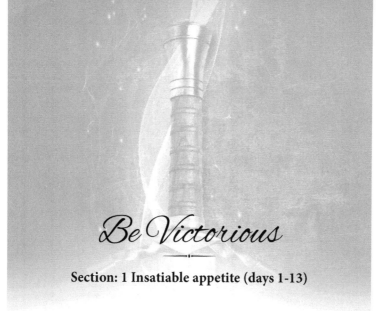

Be Victorious

Section: 1 Insatiable appetite (days 1-13)

"Then Jesus was led by the Spirit into the wilderness to be tempted by the devil. After fasting forty days and forty nights, he was hungry. The tempter came to him and said, 'If you are the Son of God, tell these stones to become bread.' Jesus answered, 'It is written: "Man shall not live on bread alone, but on every word that comes from the mouth of God."' (Matthew 4:1-4 NIV)

I don't know how long you can go without food before you get hungry, but most of us eat three times a day. Jesus was in the midst of a fast of forty days, so it's no surprise that he was hungry. Neither is it any real surprise that the enemy was going to tempt him in the area where he was currently most vulnerable – his hunger. The enemy tempted Jesus to satisfy his appetite by turning stone into bread. Just imagine the smell of that baked bread…

In this section we will be looking at some of the cravings we're tempted to satisfy, such as people-pleasing, gossiping, worrying and striving. We will explore how we can be victorious, not simply by avoiding these temptations, but by overcoming them.

To defend himself, Jesus turned to the words that came from the mouth of God, and so shall we.

DAY 1:
ARMED AND READY

"For the Lord grants wisdom! From his mouth come knowledge and understanding."
(Proverbs 2:6)

Imagine a movie battle scene between a hero and a villain; good against evil. It's taking place in a dark, dingy basement. The music is tense, disturbing, enhancing the terror of the scene. The hero waits. He can hear the sound of his enemy approaching, but he is hidden in the darkness. We watch as, undetected, the villain creeps up close, ready to kill the hero and so destroy that which is good. The impending conflict has us on the edge of our seats. Suddenly, someone throws a switch and the lights come on, piercing the darkness. Evil is exposed. Now good and evil confront one another in full view. We gasp as we note that only the villain is properly armed for battle. Surely the outcome of this scenario is not going to be good!

The psalmist describes the word of God as, *"a lamp to guide my feet and a light for my path"* (Psalm 119:105). The Word of God is a light to illuminate our path – the only way to see the route we should take. But to only use it to light up the right path surely means that, sometimes, as in the scene described above, we suddenly become aware of the dangerous position our enemy has secured; that, in fact, we are very vulnerable to attack.

This would be true if the word of God was simply a supersonic torch! But it is so much more. Jesus knew it in the wilderness and we can know it too. The word of God is not just our light, it is also our weapon.

"For the word of God is alive and powerful. It is sharper than the sharpest two-edged sword, cutting between soul and spirit, between joint and marrow. It exposes our innermost thoughts and desires." (Hebrews 4:12)

A double-sided sword is fashioned to both defend and attack. God's word is a weapon that can cut between truths and lies like a sword cuts between joints and marrow. It is a sword that can separate that which is of God and that which is of the enemy. A sword so powerful that even the secret things of our hearts and minds – that most vulnerable of battle grounds – can be exposed.

When Jesus faced the enemy in the wilderness, and his mind was bombarded by tactical temptations, he used the word of God to not only light the path he was to take, but also to defend himself. It was the best weapon available to defeat the schemes of the enemy. Jesus knew that this battle was not purely a physical one – all about his hunger – it was also a spiritual battle.

Similarly, Paul wrote to the believers in Ephesus to remind them that the battles they faced – that we still face today – were not really about physical, human issues as they appeared – they were much more sinister than that. He urged believers to,

"Be strong in the Lord and in his mighty power. Put on all of God's armour so that you will be able to stand firm against all strategies of the devil. For we are not fighting against flesh-and-blood enemies, but against evil rulers and authorities of the unseen world, against

mighty powers in this dark world, and against evil spirits in the heavenly places." (Ephesians 6: 1-12)

Paul encourages them to put on all the pieces of "spiritual armour", not leaving out a single piece which would leave them exposed. The final part of his instruction to be fully equipped with the armour of God is to, *"take the sword of the Spirit, which is the Word of God"* (Ephesians 6:18).

Throughout the Bible we see this combination of spiritual and practical readiness to do battle. In the Old Testament, Nehemiah was a man on a mission. He took a career break from being the trusted cup-bearer to King Artaxerxes to leave his exiled settlement and return to Jerusalem, to lead the reconstruction work of the city walls. He was motivated by compassion for the predicament of the repatriated Israelites. The whole book of Nehemiah is a fascinating read; when it comes to being battle-ready there are some key insights.

As well as establishing trumpeters in lookout positions, to warn the people of any impending attack, Nehemiah also armed his workers:

"The labourers carried on their work with one hand supporting their load and one hand holding a weapon. All the builders had a sword belted to their side." (Nehemiah 4:17-18)

Furthermore, Nehemiah said, *"During this time, none of us— not I, nor my relatives, nor my servants, nor the guards who were with me—ever took off our clothes. We carried our weapons with us at all times, even when we went for water."* (Nehemiah 4:23)

Even when he was off duty from his responsibilities, being refreshed or taking a break, Nehemiah remained armed and ready. I imagine that even during the night Nehemiah would have rested in a state of readiness.

Our enemy is as cunning as Nehemiah's enemies were –

constantly trying to disrupt and distract him; looking to seize every possible opportunity to attack and defeat him. That is why we too must remain vigilant and ready to do battle – not armed with the weapons of the world, but with the weapon of the Word, the ultimate sword.

Living armed and ready is essential to our journey to victory in life. That means knowing what the word of God says, and knowing how to wield it in our defence is both our priority and our victory cry. As we grow as disciples of Christ we need to grow in knowing His truth, held in the pages of the word of God. In these truths there is freedom and victory, as Jesus said.

So today, let God turn the light on to show you which path to take. Pick up His sword and keep practicing with it, so that you are ready for every eventuality. Put on your armour as Paul teaches. Like Nehemiah, keep your kit on at all times!

It is written, as Jesus said,

"You are truly my disciples if you remain faithful to my teachings. And you will know the truth, and the truth will set you free." (John 8:31-32)

———•———

Let's pray...

Father, I thank you for your Word; that it is living, sharp, double-edged, powerful and illuminating. Please help me as I begin this journey to get to know your Word more and more, so that I may remain faithful to you and what you've said. Thank you for the victory that is mine through Christ. Please help me to remain armed and ready in all seasons at all times. Amen.

DAY 2:
NO EMPTY WORDS

"Wise words are like deep waters;
wisdom flows from the wise like a bubbling brook."
(Proverbs 18:4)

Jesus was tempted to satisfy the cravings of his appetite by turning stones into bread. The real issue at stake was not hunger, of course. If he had succumbed, he would have given up his sinless nature. He would have shown God's word to be untrue – not life-giving and powerful.

In fact, God's words are so powerful that they are more satisfying than even the freshest of baked loaves. Every word of the Bible is like a seed waiting to find good soil in which to land, so that it will produce a harvest from the life contained within. God's words never fails to produce fruit – they are just waiting for the right conditions to do so. God's words also never return to him empty; they always find a landing place – a righteous heart; an open mind.

The enemy's strategy is always to cast doubt on what God has spoken into our lives through his living word. But if God has said it, then his word will come to pass.

Read the words of Isaiah the prophet:

"The rain and snow come down from the heavens and stay on the ground to water the earth. They cause the grain to grow, producing seed for the farmer and bread for the hungry. **It is the same with my word. I send it out, and it always produces fruit. It will accomplish all I want it to, and it will prosper everywhere I send it.** *You will live in joy and peace. The mountains and hills will burst into song, and the trees of the field will clap their hands! Where once there were thorns, cypress trees will grow. Where nettles grew, myrtles will sprout up. These events will bring great honour to the Lord's name; they will be an everlasting sign of his power and love."* (Isaiah 55:10-13)

As we walk with God through this book these 40 days, even when we journey through the wilderness, we will grow in confidence that the Word of God, spoken out, will bear fruit. We will discover, like Isaiah, that in place of the nettles there will be myrtles. In case you're not familiar with myrtles they are an evergreen, flowering, fruit-producing plant. In other words, instead of allowing thistles to block up our lives, God's Word will bring about life and fruitfulness every day.

Remember the story of Noah in Genesis. Noah was a righteous man, reputed to be *"the only blameless person living on earth at the time and he walked in close fellowship with God"* (Genesis 6:9). What a reputation! Noah had set himself apart for God, and was therefore set apart by God for salvation when all others perished. It was through the bloodline of Noah that the earth was repopulated.

When the rains came they poured and poured; no longer bringing nourishing life to the ground, but a wave of cleansing destruction. For forty days and forty nights the earth was pelted with water until the ground could no longer absorb it, and was flooded instead. Eventually, the rainy season did stop, but it was a long time before the aftermath died down. Isn't that often the case in our lives? Problems can sometimes seem to come from every direction in overwhelming volume. After the storm has finally abated, there are still consequences, even casualties, to contend with.

When the waters were calm, Noah sent out a raven, then a dove, to search for any hint that the land was reappearing. Twice the dove flew out, before eventually bringing back a fresh olive leaf; a sign of dry land and of grace. The dove flew until it was able to settle on a tree and bring back to Noah the signs that life was being revealed again. The fruit that had been hidden was beginning to be revealed and the dove didn't come back empty-beaked.

Just as those birds scanned the landscape, looking for somewhere to land, so God's Word looks for receptive hearts; hearts softened by the rains of life, ready to accept the seed of his word and bear fruit. Let's prepare our hearts so that his words will find a place to settle within us, to bear fruit.

God loves obedient hearts. In Deuteronomy we read a beautiful promise that was given to the people of Israel, who journeyed not for 40 days, but for 40 years through the wilderness in pursuit of the promised land. It reveals the utter love of the Lord in response to the obedience and trust of his people:

"Be careful to obey all the commands I am giving you today. Then you will live and multiply, and you will enter and occupy the land the Lord swore to give your ancestors. Remember how the Lord your God led you through the wilderness for these forty years, humbling you and testing you to prove your character, and to find out whether or not you would obey his commands. Yes, he humbled you by letting you go hungry and then feeding you with

manna, a food previously unknown to you and your ancestors. He did it to teach you that people do not live by bread alone; rather, we live by every word that comes from the mouth of the Lord." (Deuteronomy 8:1-3)

So today, consider that state of your heart. Choose today to follow Jesus in obedience. Trust that his words will settle in your heart and bear much fruit as he delights in you.

It is written,

"Now if you will obey me and keep my covenant, you will be my own special treasure from among all the peoples on earth; for all the earth belongs to me." (Exodus 19:5)

———————

Let's pray…

Lord, I thank you that even when the rains of life's trials come, I know they will pass, and afterwards there will be signs of hope and new life. Lord, soften my heart, so that I will be ready to receive every word you want to speak to me. I long for every word you speak over me to settle and bear fruit. I long to know you and walk with you as your treasure and delight. Lord, today give me the strength to obey you and follow you in my thoughts, words and actions. Amen.

DAY 3:
POWER-UP

"I love all who love me. Those who search will surely find me."
(Proverbs 8:17)

Last year I went on a guided retreat led by a friend of mine, with a focus on freedom and healing. I had set apart two days for it and was expectant that it was going to be good – especially since it came at a particularly intense time in my ministry. The retreat centre wasn't far away and the journey there should have been a simple one. But it turned out to be a much longer (and way more expensive) journey than I'd anticipated.

As I travelled down the motorway, I noticed it was feeling a little cool so I turned the heating up. I'm not one to enjoy a cold winter's drive! After a while, however, although the dial showed hot, I couldn't feel any increase in heat. Then I noticed that my accelerator didn't seem as responsive as normal and wasn't sustaining its power. I'm no mechanic, but even I could tell that something was wrong. I figured (wrongly) that I could reach my destination OK, at which point I could get the car checked over. Unfortunately, not many seconds after I'd had this thought the power went completely and I had to carefully drift across the motorway in order to grind to a halt at the edge of the tarmac. There was no safe layby to occupy. Did I also mention that this was the M25 during morning rush hour? At least that meant that the traffic was going slowly. I phoned for breakdown assistance and then waited for help.

The cavalry arrived in a matter of minutes, but not the help I'd called for. The motorway police had observed my plight and immediately came to get me out of the car and into a safer position. I had considered that given the speed of the traffic (at a virtual standstill) I was perfectly safe in my car, but the police insisted. Interestingly, as soon as I'd left my car and moved to safer ground it seemed like the traffic began to pick up speed.

Stepping back from a situation can give us a bigger perspective. From my new vantage point it became apparent that the car was in a precarious blind spot, where traffic could easily have hit me. In due course the car-rescue truck arrived, but it was not good news. Although I eventually made it to the retreat, my car did not. The engine was wrecked and the car's future was simply as scrap!

Later that evening, worshiping the Lord at the retreat, I felt the Father speak to me. My driving experience was just about to become a very expensive lesson from the Lord. He revealed that what had been going on in my car was also going on in me! My temperature was going from hot to cold. I was no longer able to express the love of the Father all the time, being more concerned about what others thought about me than I was about the Father's heart towards me. My power was becoming restricted as I was beginning to do things in my strength and not in His. Furthermore, the areas of my spiritual life that I thought were quite safe, were in fact in peril and I needed to hastily move up to higher ground.

God wanted to get to work on me. Like my car, this would

not be a quick patch-up job, but a whole renewal. The Lord had deliverance, healing and a whole new mind set in His plans for me.

Paul wrote to Timothy saying,

"I remind you to fan into flames the spiritual gift God gave you when I laid my hands on you. For God has not given us a spirit of fear and timidity, but of power, love, and self-discipline." (2 Timothy 1:6-7)

When we allow the power of the Holy Spirit and the love of the Lord to flow through us, it enables us to be the people God intends us to be. We can then practise spiritual discipline to not let either of these become of secondary importance.

Paul continued instructing Timothy:

"For God saved us and called us to live a holy life. He did this, not because we deserved it, but because that was his plan from before the beginning of time—to show us his grace through Christ Jesus. And now he has made all of this plain to us by the appearing of Christ Jesus, our Saviour. He broke the power of death and illuminated the way to life and immortality through the Good News." (2 Timothy 1:9-10)

The enemy would like nothing more than for us to live in fear and timidity; hiding in shame, quaking in inadequacy, overwhelmed by oppression. But this is not what Christ died for. He died, rose again and sent His Holy Spirit to be in us and with us. His Spirit is gifting us with power, love and self-discipline.

Being confident in the Living Word of God will enable us to be confident and victorious in all spheres of life.

When Jesus was training His disciples He said that, *"anyone who believes in me will do the same works I have done, and even greater works, because I am going to be with the Father"* (John 14:12). Dr Luke records Jesus' last audible words when He told them, *"I will send the Holy Spirit, just as my Father promised. But stay in the city until the Holy Spirit comes and fills you with power from heaven"* (Luke 24:49).

So the power that comes from Heaven by the Holy Spirit will enable us to act in the same way Jesus did; to have the same abilities Jesus had and to be able to impact the lives of others in the same way He did.

Let's not keep ploughing on in a vehicle that is just about to breakdown. Or remain in a place where we think we are safe, when we're actually in danger. Let's go up to the higher ground as we draw near to Jesus, so that like Timothy, we might fan into flame God's gift of power, love and self-discipline.

As it is written,

"Nothing in all creation will ever be able to separate us from the love of God that is revealed in Christ Jesus our Lord." (Romans 8:39)

————•————

Let's pray…

Father, I thank you for your inseparable love and your insurmountable power that enables me to have no fear, but to live a life of power, love and self-discipline. Amen.

DAY 4:
SELF-CONTROL

—•—

"Lazy people want much but get little, but those who work hard
will prosper."
(Proverbs 13:4)

We're going to continue where we left off yesterday, with the truth
that, *"God has not given us a spirit of fear and timidity, but of*
power, love and self-discipline." (2 Timothy 1:7)

I'm not sure about you, but self-discipline, or self-control, are
not my favourite words! They seem to be about restrictions, about
going without; things which in our culture tend to be negatives.
After all, we live in a culture that encourages us to believe that we
can have all things, do all things, and enjoy all things.

Paul explained to the Galatians that the fruit of having the Holy
Spirit living within us was, *"love, joy, peace, patience, kindness,*
goodness, faithfulness, gentleness and self-control" (Galatians 5:22-
23). Is it just me, or does self-control sound a little less delicious
than the other expressions of the Holy Spirit's fruit? Perhaps
it's because, apart from self-control, they all sound like pluses,
positive gains. Self-control sounds like a minus, a negative.

However, the fruit of the Spirit is not a spiritual pick 'n' mix. It's not like a fruit bowl – where we can select the fruit that appeals to us (our favourite type of apple) and discard the fruit that doesn't (like a kiwi!). Staying with the fruit analogy, the fruit of the Spirit is more like an orange – a whole entity made up of a number of complementary segments. Not having self-control in the mix would be like peeling an orange and finding that one segment was missing. It would be odd. What we would have would be an incomplete orange!

Self-control is a vital fruit of the Spirit because it keeps us anchored. It enables our roots to keep growing in Christ, so that all the other fruit can be demonstrated in our lives. Self-control will help us to *choose* to express kindness gently, goodness faithfully, love joyfully, and peace patiently.

Self-control will determine what comes *out* of our life, and will influence what we allow *into* our life. It has an effect not just on what we do, but also what we think about, what we read and watch.

Self-control is what holds us back from saying those words of retaliation to our grumpy neighbour who has just moaned at us for no good reason. Self-control means we don't have to have the last word in every disagreement. Self-control stops us from speaking out lies about ourselves or anyone else. Self-control gets us to put on our walking shoes and get moving to build up our muscles and grow in strength. Self-control will get us to turn off the screen and go to bed when we're tired, rather than falling asleep on the sofa. Self-control will get us out of bed in the morning and help us say to the Lord, "Let your will be done today." Self-control will enable the power and love of the Holy Spirit to be on display in us for the world to see.

Self-control adds so much to our life. Perhaps it should become our favourite fruit of choice!

When I was a young child my parents made a significant career change and bought a small hotel. If you've seen the British classic sitcom *Fawlty Towers*, you're close to understanding what my home environment was like. I jest of course … or do I?

Over the years, thousands of different people came and went, staying in the rooms, dining in the restaurant, drinking in the bar and relaxing in the lounge. Thousands of people were given a key and welcomed into their home away from home. Before the days of key-cards or digital passes hotel bedrooms all had their own unique keys. That meant that one person in the hotel held ultimate authority – the holder of the Master Key. With that key, no door was impassable.

Learning to exercise self-control is very much like wielding the master key. It allows us to keep secure so many doors into and out of our lives. This is why self-control is a particular battle ground that the enemy seeks to fight us on.

When Paul wrote to the believers in Rome talking about his own struggles with sin, recognising the tension in the battle for self-control, he said,

"I want to do what is right, but I can't. I want to do what is good, but I don't. I don't want to do what is wrong, but I do it anyway. But if I do what I don't want to do, I am not really the one doing wrong; it is sin living in me that does it. I have discovered this principle of life—that when I want to do what is right, I inevitably do what is wrong. I love God's law with all my heart. But there is another power within me that is at war with my mind. This power makes me a slave to the sin that is still within me. Oh, what a miserable person I am! Who will free me from this life that is dominated by sin and death? Thank God! The answer is in Jesus Christ our Lord." (Romans 7:18-25)

The answer is Jesus Christ. Paul recognised that for his personal battle in self-control the answer is actually Jesus Christ Himself.

Today, remember that because the Holy Spirit is living within you, self-control is not out of reach. Put your self-control in the hands of Jesus and let Him be the one who helps you, shows you, strengthens you and enables you. This is why Paul was able to say to Timothy,

*"For God has not given us a spirit of fear and timidity, but of power, love, and **self-discipline**."* (2 Timothy 1:7)

—————•—————

Let's pray...

Father, I thank you that your Holy Spirit fills us so that we can live with power, love and self-discipline. Lord, I thank you that you, Jesus, are the only hope for me to be able to live a life that pleases the Father. I thank you that you can help me in my weakness to make choices that will glorify you. Lord, today please help me to remember that I'm not a victim to "no control" but I am filled with heaven's power, and love and self-control.

DAY 5:
THE WEIGHT OF WAITING

"Trust in the Lord with all your heart: do not depend on your own understanding."
(Proverbs 3:5)

Do you like waiting for things? Recently I was in an automated phone queue, listening to the frustratingly repetitive music, interrupted only by a pre-recorded voice saying "Your call is important to us ... thank you for your patience ... we will be with you shortly..." The trouble was, the more I was thanked for my patience the more impatient I actually felt! Waiting was becoming increasingly stressful.

Extended times of waiting can become increasingly disappointing, as the writer of Proverbs observes:

"Hope deferred makes the heart sick, but a dream fulfilled is a tree of life." (Proverbs 13:12)

Some early gynaecological difficulties in my life left me aware that my fertility might be challenged. I therefore approached our family planning with less complacency than I might have otherwise, and much more prayerfully. Although our first daughter was conceived after just five months, I then suffered secondary-infertility and an extended season of waiting.

Both Tim and I wanted another child and our growing toddler became a persistent prompt that a sibling would be nice (a prompt that I admit to reminding her of whenever her siblings test her patience!) We both felt that having more children was a part of God's plan for us. Then there was the one occasion when a visiting preacher, who was speaking about something completely different, paused mid-sentence, looked at me and said, "You are asking for a child, but the Lord will give you *children*." Tim had to rapidly get his head around the idea that our plan for a total of two children might not be the Lord's plan for us. To further underline things, Tim had a memorable "God-dream" one night and woke up saying that he knew the name of our next two children!

It is a wonderful thing to be able to hear the Lord so clearly, yet the path still seemed so difficult to walk as weeks turned to months and then years. Every month we faced disappointment when our prayers were not answered. We began to pray for the children God told us He would give us. We prayed for them every day, for over two years.

A breakthrough came in my heart when I realised that waiting for children was not so much about me, but about my children. I realised that the words of David's well-known psalm were just as true for my unborn children as they were for me:

"You saw me before I was born. Every day of my life was recorded in your book. Every moment was laid out before a single day had passed." (Psalm 139:16)

My days were laid out before God before I was born. So were my children's. It mattered to God who they were, where they would go to school, who they would journey through life with. The details of their lives were just as significant to God as mine were to Him.

I realised that my waiting for the children was not designed to frustrate me, punish me, ignore me or overlook me. Rather it was because it was simply not the right timing. It wasn't yet God's time for them to emerge. In the waiting, I had to learn to not get in the way of the Lord's purposes by making it all about me.

Eventually, after five and a half years from the birth of our first child, Bethany, Hannah was born. Then, after a speedy twenty-one months, David was born. Our family was complete! There were no more dreams of further children. Of course, with two young kids in the house there was not much sleep to have the chance of any dreams either!

When we have God-given dreams, we need to recognise that they are not just about us! True God-given dreams are more about what God wants to do in the *fulfilment* of the dream.

Remember the famous dreamer, Joseph. He had a number of divinely inspired dreams, but made the mistake of thinking that they were all about him. As a result, he boasted to his family that they would all be bowing down to him in due course. Now, in the end they did – but not until many years had passed. Through waiting, imprisonment and hard work Joseph came to realise that the point of the dream wasn't that his family would bow down to him – it was about God positioning Joseph to elevate His purposes and move His people where He wanted them to be. Joseph's dreams were much bigger than himself. When his brothers finally did bow to him, Joseph understood so much more:

"I am Joseph, your brother, whom you sold into slavery in Egypt. But don't be upset, and don't be angry with yourselves for selling me to this place. It was God who sent me here ahead of you to preserve your lives. This famine that has ravaged the land for two years will last five more years, and there will be neither ploughing nor harvesting. God has sent me ahead of you to keep you and your

families alive and to preserve many survivors. So it was God who sent me here, not you! And he is the one who made me an adviser to Pharaoh—the manager of his entire palace and the governor of all Egypt." (Genesis 45:4-8)

As the apostle Peter reflected,

"The Lord isn't really being slow about his promise, as some people think. No, he is being patient for your sake. He does not want anyone to be destroyed, but wants everyone to repent." (2 Peter 3:9)

The Lord was so patient with the immaturity and self-centredness of Joseph. The Lord was even more patient with the selfishness and impatience I displayed.

What are you waiting for? What dreams have you had that have not yet been fulfilled?

Today, give God your dreams again and ask Him to give you His. Allow God show you how to be victorious in the waiting. Hear the voice from heaven whisper to you that you are important to God. You matter to Him. Your wait might be because there is a much bigger picture being worked out. Stand firm and do not let the enemy discourage you. Do not let him convince you that you do not matter to the Lord or that your prayers go unheard.

It is written,

"The steadfast love of the Lord never ceases; his mercies never come to an end; they are new every morning; great is your faithfulness.

'The Lord is my portion,' says my soul, 'therefore I will hope in him.'

The Lord is good to those who wait for him, to the soul who seeks him. It is good that one should wait quietly for the salvation of the Lord." (Lamentations 3:22-26 ESV)

———•———

Let's pray...

Lord, in my waiting might I not lose hope and allow disappointment to build resentment. Lord, please keep my heart soft. You are enough for me. Thank you for your mercies and faithfulness every day. I choose to trust you in the big picture with every small detail in the wait. Lord, may I be victorious in the waiting.

DAY 6:
MASTERPIECES DON'T STRIVE

—·—

"I (Wisdom) was the architect at his side. I was his constant
delight, rejoicing always in his presence.."
(Proverbs 8:30)

In the wilderness Jesus was tempted to satisfy his natural human
hunger for food – and yet it was a trap. For us, having an appetite
for craving the approval of others can be another enemy trap.

"Fear" is normally understood to refer to that horrible feeling
that rises in our gut in response to a threat (whether real or
imagined), imminent danger, pain or distress. But often in the
Bible fear is the word used to describe an awe or wonder when
considering someone far greater than us, usually God. Hence
the writer of Proverbs tells us that the, *"Fear of the Lord is the*
foundation of wisdom. Knowledge of the Holy One results in good
judgment" (Proverbs 9:10).

One of the biggest dangers we face, then, is not the fear of
imminent danger, but of misplaced awe.

We live in a culture where we often find ourselves craving
the approval of others. Young children will burst into tears in
the playground when someone tells them they don't like them

anymore or they are no longer their friend. Most people, from an early age, *want* to be liked. This follows through into adult life. Childish, daisy-petal-pulling, they-love-me, they-love-me-not, is superseded today by our apparent popularity on social media platforms. Are we getting enough likes or re-tweets? Have you ever been disappointed at how few people noticed or commented on your Facebook post? Have you longed for greater affirmation from your Instagram followers?

The paradox of social media (that by being social we somehow become more inward looking), means that more than ever before people are trying to win the approval of others; craving their affirmation so that we can be certain of our identity as a valued person. We are literally falling into the enemy's trap. The opinions of others, dealt with healthily, can help us grow and become the best version of ourselves. But not when we allow those opinions to shape our identity over and above the opinion that God has of us.

Several years ago, on a holiday with my extended family, my father came to me with an apparent "box of treasures". Inside the scruffy box were some of my childhood memorabilia that he had discovered in the back of some cupboard. It didn't seem right that I was still cluttering up their home when I could be cluttering up my own, so the box was passed over and I began the rummage down memory lane.

Amongst the various items, mostly connected with my school days, were some school reports. On most of the pages was the phrase, "Helen could do better if she tried harder". The teachers were trying, with perhaps limited success, to point out how I could reach my potential. In terms of academic achievement, this is surely a fair comment – work harder and you'll get somewhere. But we mustn't apply such thinking to our appetite for approval. Too many of us are trying harder to be liked, to be approved of, to be accepted. Before we know it, our whole identity is wrapped up in an insatiable appetite for approval, and so we begin to strive. The "fear" of others is beginning to take over and we are becoming trapped.

Some time later, when the holiday was over and the reports were cluttering up their new home in my loft, I felt the Lord challenge me about my tendency to strive. I had fallen into the trap of working hard to prove my worth, striving to be good at my job, trying hard so that I could do better! Childhood motivations were becoming adult limitations.

Notice that when Jesus was tempted by the enemy, the Father had only just affirmed Jesus as His beloved Son, following His baptism. Now the enemy was trying to get Jesus to prove His very identity through actions – as if Jesus could earn His identity for fear of showing the Father to be a liar.

I found I was so busy striving to show others I could do things, that I was blocking the Father from showing what He could do through me. If everything was being achieved by my effort, then nothing was by His grace and Spirit. Striving to prove who we are restricts the Father from displaying who He is in our life.

It's time to be free from the temptation to prove our worth. Let's no longer strive to be victorious in our own strength. Instead, we must realise that we do all things as if for the Lord, because He is our Master and we are His. As Paul said to the Colossians;

"Work willingly at whatever you do, as though you were working for the Lord rather than for people. Remember that the Lord will give you an inheritance as your reward, and that the Master you are serving is Christ." (Colossians 3:23)

Let's remind ourselves again of what Christ has done for us:

"God saved you by his grace when you believed. And you can't take credit for this; it is a gift from God. Salvation is not a reward

for the good things we have done, so none of us can boast about it. For we are God's masterpiece. He has created us anew in Christ Jesus, so we can do the good things he planned for us long ago." (Ephesians 2:8-10)

There is a beautiful freedom that comes when we recognise we can do good things because we are God's masterpiece. It is what He can do through us that enables us to do amazing things, not simply our own ability.

Praying to be released from trying to win the approval of others by impressing them with my effort released me from striving. In exchange, I received a freedom to work hard because of the gift of grace through Jesus Christ, and to let my life show who the Father is.

A masterpiece of art does not need to strive to prove itself. Instead, it displays the genius of its creator by just being itself.

Jesus had nothing to prove. He simply just had to be.

Let's not consider the approval of people more important than the love of God our Father. Let's give thanks for the gift of salvation through Jesus that means we are God's masterpieces.

As the Word of God declares,

"We are God's masterpiece. He has created us anew in Christ Jesus, so we can do the good things he planned for us long ago." (Ephesians 2:10)

———•———

Let's pray...

Father, you say that I am your masterpiece. It is because of Jesus Christ that I can do good things with my life that line up with your will for me. Today, Lord, I choose to live in the freedom of knowing who you are. May you release me from trying to earn my worth through the things that I do, and instead celebrate my worth in you because of what you have done for me, through me and in me. I am your masterpiece because of Jesus and I thank you for that. Amen.

DAY 7:
TASTE YOUR INHERITANCE

—•—

"A person without self-control is like a city with broken-down walls."
(Proverbs 25:26)

Years before Jesus spent time in a wilderness, the Israelites had been tempted with food in their own. As they wandered around, the Lord provided daily Manna. He gave very clear instructions that people were not to take more than was required for their family's daily needs. Ignoring this and being greedy resulted in a stinking maggot infestation as wasted food rotted. The Lord was teaching His children to trust Him with their food provision on a daily basis.

In another story involving the wilderness, some fine cuisine, and a desire to satisfy hunger we see one brother get trapped when he trades with his sibling, exchanging his spiritual inheritance for nothing more than a bowl of stew!

"One day when Jacob was cooking some stew, Esau arrived home from the wilderness exhausted and hungry. Esau said to Jacob, 'I'm starved! Give me some of that red stew!' (This is how Esau got his other name, Edom, which means 'red'.) 'All right,' Jacob replied,

'but trade me your rights as the firstborn son.' 'Look, I'm dying of
starvation!' said Esau. 'What good is my birthright to me now?' But
Jacob said, 'First you must swear that your birthright is mine.' So
Esau swore an oath, thereby selling all his rights as the firstborn to
his brother, Jacob. Then Jacob gave Esau some bread and lentil stew.
Esau ate the meal, then got up and left. He showed contempt for his
rights as the firstborn." (Genesis 25:29-34)

Food was a gift from God. In the Garden of Eden, however,
it became, and remains today, a significant temptation to a
number of us. When we consider the national obesity challenge,
the incessant reinvention of diets, and our general desire to
eat for a variety of reasons, not just for the sake of hunger, the
enemy knows an easy battle when he sees it. However, we can be
completely victorious in our lifestyle and habits with food, just as
Jesus showed.

When I was in my very early twenties and in my final year
of college, I felt that there were certain things that were out of
control in my life. These were triggered by a broken relationship
and like many other young people, I began to try to control what
I could. One thing I was able to control was what I ate and I began
to realise that I liked the result of losing weight. For almost a year
I significantly restricted what I ate and I made sure that not much
of what actually went in would add to my weight. Furthermore, if
I slipped and ate too much on any occasion, I would make myself
sick afterwards. I swung between harsh denial and, at other times,
eating compulsively to try and comfort some buried hurt. My
eating habits became chaotic and what I thought I was in control
of was actually beginning to control me. I was becoming trapped
in the enemy's scheme and he was set on my destruction.

I've journeyed with many people over the years who have
battled similar eating disorders and they have consistently

benefited from medical intervention. Some battles in the mind really become strongholds, but there are mental health experts that should be listened to, because they can really help.

My experience, however, was not so much a process of recovery, but of a dramatic revelation of love. It happened one afternoon when I was kneeling on my bathroom floor in my student house, hands clasped to the toilet seat whilst I emptied the contents of my stomach into the pan. Standing up with my clammy face and smudged mascara I caught a glance of myself in the bathroom mirror. In the eyes of the broken young woman staring back at me I suddenly saw the eyes of Jesus looking with a piercing, deep love right into me. I knew that His Father was my Father. He loved me with an unending love. In my tears I saw His tears. I was not just doing this to me. I was doing this to Him.

I fell back down on my knees on the bathroom floor. The tears were streaming now. Not from pain and self-recrimination but through repentance. I was allowing God's daughter to be abused and it needed to stop. Completely loved as I was, my weaknesses and all, I accepted His compassionate grace and forgiveness. I rose from that battle ground victorious. Receiving His Holy Spirit enabled me to make a promise that I would never behave like this again. And I never have.

When I came to Jesus I was given the rights of a child of God to know liberty and freedom and His loving grace in my life. I had traded that inheritance and become entrapped with food, allowing my eating habits to define who I was. It could have been any self-absorbing habit. The enemy would like nothing more than for us to give up our right to freedom in Christ by getting us to focus on our momentary desires and how we might satisfy them. However, we can rise victorious. Being a child of God doesn't exempt us from normal human appetites – all of which are part of God's grand design – but with the Holy Spirit's help we are able to submit our life to our Heavenly Father and put Him first. Simply put: It is God first, so let the "plate" wait!

Wise self-control is submitting to the Holy Spirit within us, not succumbing to controlling ourselves, so that with our bodies we can glorify God and be victorious.

It is time to recognise the battle-ground that rages around our appetites. Recognise where your areas of vulnerability lie and make a decision to stand victorious in freedom and self-control. Stand up, look in your Father's eyes, and see what He has done for you. He loves you just as you are. Today, consider your inheritance as a child of God. What are you tempted to trade it for? Freedom is yours to be received, so choose not to give it away to the enemy.

For it is written,

"Don't you realise that your body is the temple of the Holy Spirit, who lives in you and was given to you by God? You do not belong to yourself, for God bought you with a high price. So you must honour God with your body." (1 Corinthians 6:19-20)

———•———

Let's pray...

Father, I thank you for your love and the price you paid for me through Jesus. Today may I honour you in my life by honouring the body you've given me and make choices that bless you and please you. May I live free and victorious and realise that above all else I depend upon you. May I glorify you even in the choices of what I eat. Amen.

DAY 8:
WORRY

———•———

"Worry weighs a person down' an encouraging word cheers a person up."
(Proverbs 12:25)

If Jesus had given in to the temptation to meet His own needs, to satisfy His own appetite, He would have shown a lack of trust in His Father as His provider. The enemy was tempting Jesus to worry about whether God would really come through for Him.

When we allow our thinking to be consumed with satisfying our own needs, we can be drawn into a snare of worry. The activity of worry is defined as *tormenting oneself with, or suffering from, disturbing thoughts.* Surely no one would intentionally torment themselves? Yet, sadly, many do. A great many are suffering from worry and anxiety.

The first thoughts that bombarded Jesus' mind, tempting Him to satisfy His appetite for food Himself, bypassing the will of His Father, were obviously not sin, because Jesus never sinned. It was just temptation, and temptation isn't sin. When we don't stop at that first thought and deal with problem – that's when things begin to go wrong and we begin to be sucked into sin's trap.

At it's heart, worry is a lack of trust. It questions the character of God and doubts that He will come through for us when we need Him. Jesus was very clear when He spoke to His disciples and a gathered crowd about worry.

"Can all your worries add a single moment to your life? And if worry can't accomplish a little thing like that, what's the use of worrying over bigger things? Look at the lilies and how they grow. They don't work or make their clothing, yet Solomon in all his glory was not dressed as beautifully as they are. And if God cares so wonderfully for flowers that are here today and thrown into the fire tomorrow, he will certainly care for you. Why do you have so little faith? And don't be concerned about what to eat and what to drink. Don't worry about such things. These things dominate the thoughts of unbelievers all over the world, but your Father already knows your needs. Seek the Kingdom of God above all else, and he will give you everything you need." (Luke 12:25-31)

Stopping worrying means taking our eyes off our needs and looking towards the One who really knows what we need. Maybe we can't flick a switch in our heads, but we can choose to shift our focus. Instead of looking at your self, look at Jesus instead.

Paul tackles this same temptation to sin when he speaks to the believers in Philippi:

"Don't worry about anything; instead, pray about everything. Tell God what you need, and thank him for all he has done. Then you will experience God's peace, which exceeds anything we can understand. His peace will guard your hearts and minds as you live in Christ Jesus. And now, dear brothers and sisters, one final thing. Fix your thoughts on what is true, and honourable, and right, and pure, and lovely, and admirable. Think about things that are excellent and worthy of praise. Keep putting into practice all you learned and received from me—everything you heard from me and

saw me doing. Then the God of peace will be with you." (Philippians 4:6-9)

Don't *worry*. Instead pray about everything.

Worry is us talking to ourselves and going round and round in circles, tormenting ourselves. Prayer is talking to our loving Father and giving everything to Him, trusting Him with ourselves and all our needs and concerns.

Several years ago I was going to make my first trip to visit some dear friends and ministry partners of ours in Burkina Faso, West Africa. They had stayed in our home on numerous occasions and my husband Tim and various teams from our church had visited them on numerous occasions. However, the night before I was due to fly, a thought came into my mind that I would never come home again and never see my children. Instead of immediately turning this concern over to the Lord and trusting Him with my life, and that of my children, I allowed this thought to torment me. And I really did become tormented. I could not finish a sentence without crying. I was literally inconsolable. When I finally lay down to go to sleep my exasperated husband, who is a seasoned traveller, simply said there were no more words he could use to console me, so I should just try and trust the Lord. He rolled over and went to sleep, whilst I cried myself to sleep, gripped with fear.

I would like to say that I woke up victorious and went on the trip full of confidence. The truth is, however, that I was still weeping as I headed to the airport. Worry was tormenting me and worse still I was partnering with it.

Eventually, as I fastened my seat belt on the plane and realised there was no turning back, I finally gave my life and the life of my most dearly loved ones, over to the Lord. Peace filled my heart and I was ready to go. The trip was amazing and I loved every minute of it. I even cried when it came time to leave my dear friends in Africa and head home to my loved ones. The next trip to Burkina Faso, a year or so later, was a far less stressful affair, because I knew what to do when the enemy landed a tempting thought.

Worry will strangle the life, hope and peace out of us, but the truth of the Word of God can cut through its vice-like grip and allow peace to guard us.

One day I was having a pastoral chat with a lady from my church family. She was completely overwhelmed with worry, to the point that she was now literally worrying about worrying. There seemed to be so many things available to worry about, from the progress of her young child, to the state of her marriage, the current economy and the threat of terrorism. My heart ached for the burdens she was carrying and the trap she had become ensnared in. The enemy was now able to just sit back and smile at his victim's distress. However, the word of the Lord is powerful and liberating. The beautiful moment came when instead of calling herself a worrier she began to lean into the identity of an intercessor. Instead of worrying and focussing on herself, she began to turn her thoughts prayerfully towards the Father and focus on Him.

Stopping worrying and starting to pray is not a magic trick, it is a choice. As Paul said, *"Keep putting into practice all you learned."* It is a choice which can be exercised.

Today, look for the signs of seeds of worry settling in your thoughts. Chase them off before they take root. Anxious thoughts do not need to be entertained, however small they are. Turn all these negative thoughts into a prayer and give them to God … again and again if necessary. Keep praying.

It is written:

"Give your burdens to the Lord, and he will take care of you. He

will not permit the godly to slip and fall." (Psalm 55:22)

———•———

Let's pray...

Lord, I give every one of my concerns to you (be specific and list them). *I choose to look at you Lord and how you have provided for all my needs. Lord, I thank you for all you have done for me. I thank you for...* (be specific and list them). *Lord, please help me to remain mindful of you and trust you with all my needs.*

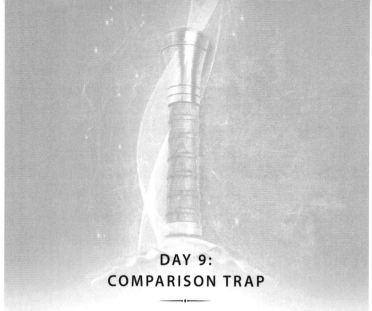

DAY 9:
COMPARISON TRAP

———•———

"Fearing people is a dangerous trap, but trusting the Lord means safety."
(Proverbs 29:25)

Another of the traps the enemy would like to lure us into is that of comparison. In a bid to feed our self-worth, we can fall into comparing ourselves to others in unhelpful ways. Our modern culture is obsessed with "entitlement". People think that they can and should have everything. Even as Christians, if we are not careful we can find our perfectly normal desire for affirmation twisted into a personal campaign for personal prosperity.

Let me explain. I have three children, each of whom is quite capable of waving the flag of unfairness if they think it will result in preferential treatment. Our youngest, David, will complain that because he is the youngest he is not treated the same as his older siblings. Our eldest, Bethany, will complain that we are not as strict with her younger siblings as we were with her. Hannah, our middle child, will complain that she is stuck in the middle of our preferred first and favoured last! They are comparing their situation to that of their siblings.

The children protest against apparent injustice and unfairness, and want to be treated fairly by their parents – which they interpret as being treated "the same" as one another. As a parent, however, I have discovered that same-ness is not always appropriate. What constitutes a reward for one child for good behaviour is not such a significant blessing for another. One discipline works for one child, but not for another, and so on. As their parent, I want to treat them fairly, but I can't commit to treating them the same.

Falling into the comparison trap means that we are constantly looking over our shoulder at other people to see how they're doing, which means we are no longer focussing on who we are meant to be. Paul used the analogy of a running race to explain it. We can't run an effective race if we spend all our time looking at how those around us are running.

Paul told his Philippian audience that there was a specific purpose for which Christ had taken hold of him. He therefore intended to press on to take hold of that purpose. He had no intention of taking hold of someone else's purpose!

"Not that I have already obtained all this, or have already arrived at my goal, but I press on to take hold of that for which Christ Jesus took hold of me." (Philippians 3:12 NIV)

Similarly, the writer to Hebrews talks about a specific race that is marked out for us. We need to keep running straight ahead, making sure that we don't drift over into someone else's lane.

"Therefore, since we are surrounded by such a great cloud of witnesses, let us throw off everything that hinders and the sin that so easily entangles. And let us run with perseverance the race marked out for us, fixing our eyes on Jesus, the pioneer and perfecter of faith. For the joy set before him he endured the cross, scorning its shame, and sat down at the right hand of the throne of God." (Hebrews 12:1-3 NIV)

Comparing our lot to someone else's is like trying to run a race with our head permanently turned to one side. I don't know if you've tried doing this, but first of all looking sideways will significantly slow you down, then it will ensure you drift off course. The world's top athletes hardly spare a sideways glance. They keep their eyes firmly fixed on the finish line, then they press on, fast and focussed.

When the disciples fell into the comparison trap, Jesus sharply corrected them. They were wondering about their future and comparing each other's prospects. *"Jesus answered, 'If I want him to remain alive until I return, what is that to you? You must follow me'"* (John 21:22 NIV).

Our eyes must be on Jesus, not on someone else.

There was a time when I followed more people on Twitter than I do now. Many were people I didn't know personally, but whose ministry I really valued. After a while though, I became aware that I wasn't just valuing their ministry, I was comparing mine to theirs. I was being lured into a comparison trap and seemed to just drift into it. My eyes slowly came off Jesus and onto them. I began to become jealous and complain to the Lord about how unfair it was that they had this opportunity or that opportunity; how they seemed more favoured. The comparison trap encouraged the fruit of jealousy to grow and this is not Kingdom fruit.

So I actively chose to un-follow some people and actively chose to follow Christ. To run my own race. To press on to take hold of the things for which Christ has taken hold of me.

We must sharpen our sword and fight the enemy's temptations with the powerful truth to be free from the comparison trap.

Today, ask yourself, are you jealous of what God seems to have done in someone else's life? Are you thinking that the lane someone else is running in looks like a better lane than yours and that's not fair? Check who you are following. Are you following Jesus in the right lane, or are you in the wrong lane?

It is written:

"'For I know the plans I have for you,' says the Lord. 'They are plans for good and not for disaster, to give you a future and a hope. In those days when you pray, I will listen. If you look for me wholeheartedly, you will find me. I will be found by you,' says the Lord." (Jeremiah 29:11-14)

———•———

Let's pray...

Lord, today I want to choose to fix my eyes on you, to seek you wholeheartedly and to live the life you have prepared for me. Help me to not look at others and compare myself to them. Help me to run my race and encourage others to run their own race. Lord, forgive me for making wrong comparisons. Today I choose to follow you.

DAY 10:
CAN I TELL YOU A SECRET?

"A gossip goes around telling secrets, but those who are trustworthy can keep a confidence"
(Proverbs 11: 13)

Many will have played the childhood game of "Chinese Whispers", where people line up and pass a whispered message from one person to the next. Eventually, the message is announced by the last recipient and the fun is in seeing how much it has altered from the original. At some point, the message will have been significantly altered, perhaps due to its complexity, because it has been misheard, spoken in a rush, or even intentionally sabotaged.

Perhaps the adult version of this game is gossip. The writer of Proverbs says that, *"The words of a whisperer are like delicious morsels; they go down into the inner parts of the body"* (Proverbs 18:8 ESV). People love to gossip! But just like Chinese Whispers, it is a poor method of communication.

Why do people gossip? Because we are frequently overcome with the desire to "know". We have to know things. Our seemingly insatiable need to know fills pages upon pages of newspaper and magazine columns, and endless social media news feeds. Most of which is about as accurately reported as a Chinese whisper, favouring cloaked conversations and scandalous status updates. Yet, people constantly swallow it as if it was the gospel truth.

Knowing something important before someone else can fill us with a false sense of power and make us feel special. Our guard should be up when someone leans close and whispers, "Don't tell anyone else, but…"

Consider the sadness of David when, as a victim of gossip, he wrote,

"But my enemies say nothing but evil about me. 'How soon will he die and be forgotten?' they ask. They visit me as if they were my friends, but all the while they gather gossip, and when they leave, they spread it everywhere. All who hate me whisper about me, imagining the worst. 'He has some fatal disease,' they say. 'He will never get out of that bed!' Even my best friend, the one I trusted completely, the one who shared my food, has turned against me." (Psalm 41:5-9)

None of us like being the subject of gossip. However, amnesia seems to set in when we are tempted to hear and share what we hear about someone else, sometimes even camouflaging it as a prayer request! We are hoodwinked into forgetting our discernment.

Have you heard the expression that *a chain is only as strong as its weakest link?* This phrase is normally used in the context of strengthening potential areas of weakness. But what if the chain were gossip? A chain of gossip could be broken by the "weakest" link – the one that doesn't pass on what is heard; the one who doesn't embellish the story or try to keep it alive. The weakest link in a gossip-chain can break the chain and end the gossip. It is time to be the weakest link!

The temptation to gossip, to be part of some inner circle, is really just an indication of something else that is happening within. As Jesus said,

"*A tree is identified by its fruit. If a tree is good, its fruit will be good. If a tree is bad, its fruit will be bad ... For whatever is in your heart determines what you say. A good person produces good things from the treasury of a good heart, and an evil person produces evil things from the treasury of an evil heart. And I tell you this, you must give an account on judgment day for every idle word you speak. The words you say will either acquit you or condemn you.*" (Matthew 12:33-37)

David, writing in the Psalms, speaks of his desire to be a man of integrity, who doesn't become a receiver or a conductor of gossip to others.

"*I will sing of your love and justice, Lord. I will praise you with songs. I will be careful to live a blameless life— when will you come to help me? I will lead a life of integrity in my own home. I will refuse to look at anything vile and vulgar. I hate all who deal crookedly; I will have nothing to do with them. I will reject perverse ideas and stay away from every evil. I will not tolerate people who slander their neighbours. I will not endure conceit and pride. I will search for faithful people to be my companions. Only those who are above reproach will be allowed to serve me. I will not allow deceivers to serve in my house, and liars will not stay in my presence.*" (Psalm 101:1-7)

Remember that we are in a spiritual battle. We need to see the strategy of the enemy when it comes to gossip so that we can confidently wield the sword of truth. Jesus explained this in no uncertain terms to a crowd of people listening to Him teach in the Temple:

"*If God were your Father, you would love me, because I have come to you from God. I am not here on my own, but he sent me.*

Why can't you understand what I am saying? It's because you can't even hear me! For you are the children of your father the devil, and you love to do the evil things he does. He was a murderer from the beginning. He has always hated the truth, because there is no truth in him. When he lies, it is consistent with his character; for he is a liar and the father of lies. So when I tell the truth, you just naturally don't believe me! Which of you can truthfully accuse me of sin? And since I am telling you the truth, why don't you believe me? Anyone who belongs to God listens gladly to the words of God. But you don't listen because you don't belong to God." (John 8:42-47)

The people were so busy with their own theories and intrigue that Jesus said, "You can't even hear me!" Today let us recognise the enemy's scheme to trap us in an insatiable appetite for gossip. He is the father of lies, so we need to turn our ears and eyes away from him. Let's choose to be "the weakest link" in the gossip chain and not listen to or read about idle gossip, whether it's about a celebrity or a friend! Let's make a choice not to pass on gossip, but instead focus on the things of God.

It is written,

"And now, dear brothers and sisters, one final thing. Fix your thoughts on what is true, and honourable, and right, and pure, and lovely, and admirable. Think about things that are excellent and worthy of praise." (Philippians 4:8)

———•———

Let's pray…

Lord, forgive me for the times when I become entangled in gossip. Today I choose to break this chain and to live a life of integrity, following you. I choose to not pursue gossip and I choose not to pass it on. For your glory. Amen.

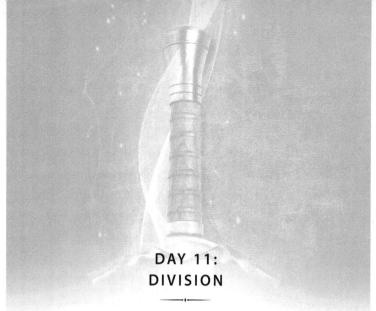

DAY 11:
DIVISION

———•———

"A gentle answer deflects anger, but harsh words make tempers flare."
(Proverbs 15:1)

One appetite we're often tempted to satisfy is the need to be right! Jesus expected His followers to be offended at some point, which is why He gave some of His most prescriptive and clear teaching ever. Taking offence is a choice, and it is an area in which the enemy loves to trap us. Our desire to be right, to be properly understood for our intentions (even if our actions are faulty) can leave us vulnerable to offence.

This might be an unusual thing to suggest, but I'd like you to consider becoming like a well-oiled duck! Not the sort that is crispy, with hoisin sauce and a little pancake, but the sort that is still swimming, fully feathered and well oiled. Although ducks spend most of their time in water, if they have preened themselves well their feathers are coated in a natural oil, so that they hardly get wet. Instead they keep dry and warm – even though they are completely surrounded by water!

We might not preen ourselves with duck-oil, but if we are filled with the oil of the Holy Spirit, then it is possible to find ourselves in potentially offensive situations and still not get offended.

Recorded in Matthew's gospel is Jesus' clear, step-by-step guide of what to do if you are hurt or offended by someone:

"If another believer sins against you, go privately and point out the offense. If the other person listens and confesses it, you have won that person back. But if you are unsuccessful, take one or two others with you and go back again, so that everything you say may be confirmed by two or three witnesses. If the person still refuses to listen, take your case to the church. Then if he or she won't accept the church's decision, treat that person as a pagan or a corrupt tax collector. I tell you the truth, whatever you forbid on earth will be forbidden in heaven, and whatever you permit on earth will be permitted in heaven. I also tell you this: If two of you agree here on earth concerning anything you ask, my Father in heaven will do it for you. For where two or three gather together as my followers, I am there among them." (Matthew 18:15-20)

What to do when someone offends us

First, Jesus tells us to go to the person direct and speak to them privately. This means that we don't tell our spouse, our best friend, a stranger at a bus-stop, or the world by posting an irate status update on Facebook. Keep the matter private and speak to the person concerned. Most issues can be solved here. Whilst all of us can, at times, be clumsy with our words and actions, generally we don't set out to hurt those whom we've offended.

I'm quite a direct talker and often do my thinking out loud. This is fine on most occasions, but there are times when my communication is not well thought-out and others have been hurt. One of my best friends for over twenty years is also someone I've worked closely with in various jobs, both inside and outside of the church. She's an incredibly gracious, gentle, yet strong lady. My friend models this process of talking in private, taking the issue direct to the person concerned. She's had to have a quiet word with me on more than one occasion, when I've spoken in a way that, sadly, has hurt her. Of course, I've never done this deliberately – honest! But as a result of her commitment, this is one of my safest friendships. I know that we will always have short accounts with one another. She won't allow any issue to fester and become septic as a result.

Of course, Jesus knows that not everyone will admit their fault quickly. Some will deny responsibility. If that happens, then and only then, should a third party be brought into the discussion – preferably someone respected by both parties with the wisdom to mediate. Then, before the world of Facebook has woken up to the situation, there is still a chance of private reconciliation.

The final stage, if all else fails and the relationship is in danger of becoming permanently fractured, it is time to go to the church and seek further help.

In over seventeen years of leading a church family I have only seen a whole church need to be involved in a dispute on one occasion. On every other occasion the issues were able to be resolved privately or with the help of a mediator. Unless, of course, Jesus' simple method was ignored and the aggrieved parties wen their separate ways. Then, tragically, I've seen many situations of pain turn into a toxic hardness of heart, where layers of hurt upon hurt weigh down a person's spirit.

Such situations need not occur. Looking beyond disputes to hoped-for unity among believers, Jesus wants us to value our relationships and live in peace together, so that our prayers will be answered:

"If two of you agree here on earth concerning anything you

ask, my Father in heaven will do it for you. For where two or three gather together as my followers, I am there among them." (Matthew 18:19-20)

Our enemy is campaigning for the complete opposite. He wants division to reign so that our prayers go unanswered. He delights when we are hurt or cause hurt.

Today, think about whether you are harbouring any hurt against someone. Or alternatively, do you know you have hurt someone else and an apology is overdue? Jesus also taught His disciples that before they came to worship in the temple, they should to make sure everything was right in their relationships with others.

"If you are presenting a sacrifice at the altar in the Temple and you suddenly remember that someone has something against you, leave your sacrifice there at the altar. Go and be reconciled to that person. Then come and offer your sacrifice to God." (Matthew 5:23-24)

Sometimes, sadly, it is impossible to make amends with people for various reasons. However, wherever possible let us choose to align with the Lord's way and be peacemakers.

It is time to be more like a well-oiled duck and to allow the Holy Spirit to help us work for peace; to restore relationships; to let go of offence. Today is the day to break free from the pain that would constrict you and begin to heal.

It is written: *"God blesses those who work for peace, for they will be called the children of God."* (Matthew 5:9-10)

―――・―――

Let's pray...

Lord, please forgive me for the times when I've hurt others (be specific with what you know) *and I ask that you would bless them and bring healing into their life. Forgive me when I've taken offence and not dealt with things in the way that you have taught me to do. Forgive me, Lord, when I talk to other people before I've talked to the one who has offended me. Lord, please help me to not be entrapped by the enemy to satisfy my right to be offended, but to give up this right and become a disciple who works for peace. Amen.*

DAY 12:
REMEMBER TO FORGIVE

"Love prospers when a fault is forgiven, but dwelling on it separates close friends."
(Proverbs 17:9)

Pointing out to someone when they have hurt you gives them a chance to say sorry, to explain themselves, and for you both to share your perspectives and ultimately restore relationships. Sometimes, however, the hurt is so deep that it requires more than a conversation to understand the other person's point of view. Instead it requires something far more significant: forgiveness.

The enemy's strategy is to keep us bound up in unforgiveness, because he knows this will rob us of intimacy in our relationship with the Heavenly Father. It's time we understood the weapon of forgiveness a little bit more.

People have lots of conflicting ideas about what forgiveness means. Phrases that people commonly use, such as *forgive and forget* only serve to muddy the waters. Forgiving someone doesn't suddenly give us amnesia. Forgiveness is not so much about forgetting, but more about remembering! Remembering what we personally have been forgiven for is often the starting place for forgiving someone else. Remembering who we have been forgiven by is the next step.

Jesus taught His disciples how to be victorious in forgiveness by telling a brilliant parable about two debtors.

Firstly there was a man, let's call him Fred, who owed the king a truck load of money. The time came when the king was asking every one who owed him money to pay up, now! But Fred realised that he couldn't afford to pay his huge debt back, so he went to the king and begged for leniency. After hearing Fred pleading, the king was filled with compassion, so he forgave him the debt. All of it! He didn't have to pay back a thing.

Fred was so relieved. He set off for home with a huge smile on his face, the heavy load lifted from his shoulders. As he was nearing home, however, Fred bumped into a man, let's call him Ted, who owed him some money. Ted owed a tiny amount compared to the debt Fred had owed to the king. Similarly, Ted didn't have any money, so he begged Fred for leniency. But Fred's heart was not moved with compassion. He was more interested in this debt being settled. So he had Ted thrown into jail until he could pay the debt in full. Of course, the king heard about all this.

"Then the king called in the man he had forgiven and said, 'You evil servant! I forgave you that tremendous debt because you pleaded with me. Shouldn't you have mercy on your fellow servant, just as I had mercy on you?' Then the angry king sent the man to prison to be tortured until he had paid his entire debt. That's what my heavenly Father will do to you if you refuse to forgive your brothers and sisters from your heart" (Matthew 18:32-35).

Before telling this story Jesus had told His disciples that if someone persisted in sinning against them, they should keep on forgiving them – seventy times seven times, if necessary, which was His way of saying there should be no limit. A person, repeatedly wronging them required repeated forgiveness – not because they were to forget what this person had done, but rather because they were to remember how much they themselves had been forgiven.

Elsewhere Jesus taught the principle, *"When someone has been given much, much will be required in return; and when someone has been entrusted with much, even more will be required"* (Luke 12:48). This applies to forgiveness too. When we consider how much we have been forgiven by the King of Heaven, we will grow in our capacity to receive His love for us, which in turn can be poured out to others.

One day Jesus was a guest at someone's house when a woman came and anointed His feet with expensive perfume, in an extravagant act of worship. Immediately He told a short parable about forgiveness.

"'A man loaned money to two people—500 pieces of silver to one and 50 pieces to the other. But neither of them could repay him, so he kindly forgave them both, cancelling their debts. Who do you suppose loved him more after that?' Simon answered, 'I suppose the one for whom he cancelled the larger debt.' ... 'I tell you, her sins— and they are many—have been forgiven, so she has shown me much love. But a person who is forgiven little shows only little love.'" (Luke 7:41-43,47)

Forgiveness doesn't make a wrong right, or remove consequences, or cause spiritual amnesia to set in. Forgiveness disarms the enemy from keeping us locked up in the pain and trauma of the offence and enables us to be filled with the Father's love. Forgiveness can be given when forgiveness has first been received, in full, from the Father.

Let's always remember, as David wrote in the Psalms:

"The Lord is compassionate and merciful, slow to get angry and

filled with unfailing love. He will not constantly accuse us, nor remain angry forever. He does not punish us for all our sins; he does not deal harshly with us, as we deserve. For his unfailing love toward those who fear him is as great as the height of the heavens above the earth. He has removed our sins as far from us as the east is from the west." (Psalm 103:8-12)

When you think about the wrong things that have been done to you, put them in the context of how much you have been forgiven. How much forgiveness have you received from the Father? Is there un-confessed sin on your part?

It is written:

"But if we confess our sins to him, he is faithful and just to forgive us our sins and to cleanse us from all wickedness." (1 John 1:9)

————·————

Let's pray...

Lord, I confess to you (be specific) *the wrong that I have done against you and I receive your forgiveness through Christ who sets me free. Father, please fill me with your love so that I might live as you desire and give forgiveness away to others, out of the abundance that I've received. I choose to forgive...* (be specific) *for all that has been done against me, and I ask you fill me afresh with your love. Amen.*

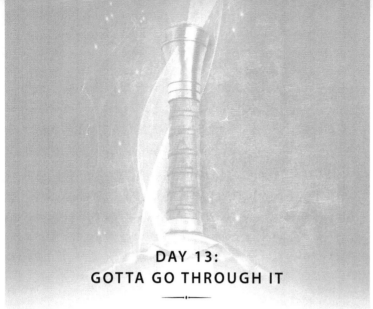

DAY 13:
GOTTA GO THROUGH IT

"You can go to bed without fear; you will lie down and sleep soundly."
(Proverbs 2:24)

We're coming to the end of the first section of this journey of victory. Jesus, led into the wilderness by the Spirit was tested for forty days. The Israelites journeyed in the wilderness too, but for forty years. Following God took the Israelites, and Jesus, into and through the wilderness, not around it. It is in the wilderness that some of our greatest victories are won; where some of our greatest encounters with the Father are experienced.

A favourite book of my children when they were young (and me if I'm honest) was *We're Going on a Bear Hunt*. A family goes looking for a bear and encounters various types of terrain, from grass to mud to a river. Each time we read that they cannot go over it, under it, or round it – they've just got to go *through* it. We used to turn our lounge into the story and create the scenes with blankets and cushions. It was fun, if I say so myself.

Following Jesus is really not the same as going on a bear hunt (in case you needed clarification), but how we handle the terrain on our journey is not dissimilar. Some things can't be bypassed, they have to be gone through. If Jesus travelled into the wilderness and got through it, then we gotta get through it too! Following Christ as His disciple does not mean that we will avoid the wilderness experiences any more than Jesus Himself did. However, it does mean that we can encounter Jesus in the wilderness.

Mark tells the story of the Lord's provision in the wilderness when, "*...another large crowd had gathered, and the people ran out of food again. Jesus called his disciples and told them, 'I feel sorry for these people. They have been here with me for three days, and they have nothing left to eat. If I send them home hungry, they will faint along the way. For some of them have come a long distance.' His disciples replied, 'How are we supposed to find enough food to feed them out here in the wilderness?'*" (Mark 8:1-4)

The disciples had obviously already forgotten that Jesus had recently fed five thousand people who had gathered to hear Him in another remote place. Once again they were perplexed and aware of their own inability to meet the needs of four thousand hungry people in the wilderness. If they'd been close to a town, perhaps they would have been more confident in rustling up a tasty feast, but here they were out of their comfort zone. There are no resources to hand. Yet Jesus took the inadequate supply of a small picnic meal, blessed it, multiplied it, gave it away and met everyone's need for food, with plenty left over!

In our lack, Jesus is our provision. Without first knowing the lack, would we really know Him as our provider? Furthermore, without knowing grief, would we know Him as our comforter? Without knowing loneliness, would we know Him as our friend? Without knowing our weakness, would we know Him as our strength?

Jesus preached this message to a large crowd in order to show them that God is well aware of our wilderness times, and that as we go through them, they are actually an opportunity to meet with the Father and see how He provides for our needs.

"God blesses those who are poor and realize their need for him, for the Kingdom of Heaven is theirs. God blesses those who mourn, for they will be comforted. God blesses those who are humble, for they will inherit the whole earth. God blesses those who hunger and thirst for justice, for they will be satisfied. God blesses those who are merciful, for they will be shown mercy. God blesses those whose hearts are pure, for they will see God. God blesses those who work for peace, for they will be called the children of God. God blesses those who are persecuted for doing right, for the Kingdom of Heaven is theirs. God blesses you when people mock you and persecute you and lie about you and say all sorts of evil things against you because you are my followers. Be happy about it! Be very glad! For a great reward awaits you in heaven." (Matthew 5:3-12)

Ezekiel's prophetic words also show the Father's plans for us as we follow Him through wilderness times. Note that because of Jesus, our relationship with the Father is made secure. We can be confident then, even in the wilderness, that He is with us. We can camp there in safety and sleep in peace.

"I will make a covenant of peace with my people and drive away the dangerous animals from the land. Then they will be able to camp safely in the wildest places and sleep in the woods without fear." (Ezekiel 34:25)

As we journey through the wilderness with Jesus, He wants to meet us in the middle of it. He's not waiting to meet us at the end, once we've emerged.

As the enemy tempted Jesus to be His own provision in a time of needs, so the enemy tempts us to be the same. But in the wilderness the Lord wants to provide everything we need.

Today, as we look ahead, can we close the gap between us and Jesus so that we're following Him even more closely? Can we walk in the footprints He leaves in front of us and cross the terrain of the wilderness staying close to Him? When He pauses we can camp safely; when we need to rest we can do so without fear; when He moves forward, we can advance. Through all our challenges we can know Him as the provider of all we need, so that even in the dry places, He fills us with His life.

It is written:

"I will make a pathway through the wilderness. I will create rivers in the dry wasteland." (Isaiah 43:18-19)

Let's pray...

Jesus, I am choosing to follow you and I know that means you might cause me to walk through some wilderness times. Lord, I trust you to lead me through. I trust that your Word will show me the path to take, even in the wilderness. Lord, you are my provider and I will not satisfy any of my selfish appetites with anything else. Lord, I trust you and I will keep following you though it all. Amen.

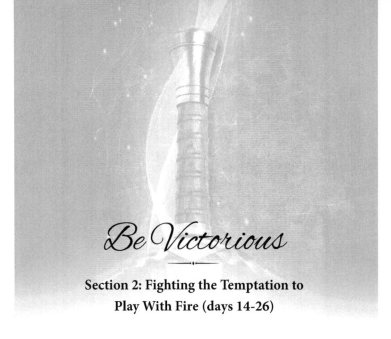

Be Victorious

Section 2: Fighting the Temptation to Play With Fire (days 14-26)

"Then the devil took him to the holy city and had him stand on the highest point of the temple. 'If you are the Son of God,' he said, 'throw yourself down. For it is written: "He will command his angels concerning you, and they will lift you up in their hands, so that you will not strike your foot against a stone."' Jesus answered him, 'It is also written: "Do not put the Lord your God to the test."'" (Matthew 4:5-7)

Bad stuff really does happen to good people. Being a Christian does not exempt us from any of this. Is it possible to journey through the storms of life, yet still be victorious? In this section we will explore how even in the storms, trials and tests, we can find peace, confidence and victory. We will explore how to deal with unanswered prayers, doubts, fears and the oft-repeated cry of our heart: "Why me?"

DAY 14:
PEACE-EXCHANGE

"He is a shield to those who walk with integrity."
(Proverbs 2:7)

When Jesus was tempted to jump from the temple heights in order to "prove" Himself, He would have leapt to His death unless He gave up His humanity. But then He would no longer be the Messiah. Jesus, however, didn't give up His humanity and as a result we are able to exchange some of ours for His Spirit. Let me explain.

We sat in the car, going nowhere. Our hands interlocked and tears streamed down our faces. Outside it was raining hard. I don't know which poured down more. All this scene needed was a string quartet in the back seat playing tense music and we would have had the perfect traumatic movie storm scene.

We were numbed by the news we'd never wanted to hear. A few minutes earlier we had been sitting in a hospital waiting room, anticipating seeing the doctor who had some test results. I was the last patient he had to see during the evening clinic. As we sat facing the doctor across his desk I noticed my name scribbled on a list, but with an asterisk highlighting it. He was the surgeon who just two weeks earlier had performed a lumpectomy on my leg. The operation had been traumatic, but he had successfully removed the mysterious lump; a lump that no one suspected was significant or sinister. Yet here we were and now the surgeon soberly informed me that I had terminal, secondary cancer.

As Tim and I sat in the car, crying, holding each other, we simply reached out to God. We choked out sincere, childlike prayers that we wanted whatever He wanted. The words tumbled with the tears, Lord, let your will be done." Almost immediately, we were overwhelmed with peace. There was no audible voice or profound revelation. We still didn't know what would happen. There was no hint of how things would shape up. Yet there was a peace. It was almost like God placed us in a bubble to protect us – one that would continue to shield us through the weeks of uncertain terrain that lay ahead.

Approximately two thousand years earlier Jesus had faced death, wrestling with the consequences of what was about to happen. He didn't want to suffer a horrible, painful death, and He wrestled in prayer, under extreme pressure, until He sweated blood. Yet He was willing, for all our sakes, to say to His heavenly father, *"Not my will, but yours be done."* Overwhelmed with peace He journeyed silently through the proceeding trauma in submission, trusting His Father for the outcome; that His Father's will would be done. Trust and submission took Him to the cross. Which, incidentally, is the place where our healing was made possible.

If I could write the script of my life I'm sure there would be a few deleted scenes which would not make the cut. At the very least I would have done a few re-writes. There are no doubt things in your life that you wish were not a part of your story. Or things you are going through right now that you wish you didn't have to go through. The enemy would love to cripple you with fear, numb you with news, introduce some suffering or seemingly interrupt all your hopes. However, today, in exchange for fear, anxiety and disappointment, the Lord wants to gift you with His overwhelming peace. This exchange is secured by the choice of *trust*. To say, as Jesus did, "Not my will but yours be done."

On day eight of this journey we looked at our appetite for worry. I remind you of Paul's words:

"Don't worry about anything; instead, pray about everything. Tell God what you need, and thank him for all he has done. Then you will experience God's peace, which exceeds anything we can understand. His peace will guard your hearts and minds as you live in Christ Jesus." (Philippians 4:6-7)

Giving up our will for His enables us to receive His peace at all times, which guards our greatest battlegrounds – our heart and mind.

Having a peace that exceeds our understanding means that even when there seems to be evidence to the contrary, we can still trust the Lord and enjoy His peace. As Tim and I went from doctor's appointment to doctor's appointment, and I had test after test, procedure after procedure, the evidence presented to us was enough to fill us with grave concern. But, surpassing all of this was a peace from heaven that protected us, guarded us, and enabled us to continue, confidently knowing that whatever the outcome, God's will would be done.

Today, pause and consider how the enemy would like to keep you gripped in fear, yet the Father wants you to exchange this for His peace. Make the exchange, as Paul showed us how. As you tell the Father your worries and thank Him for what He has done, may you be filled with peace.

It is written:

"I am leaving you with a gift—peace of mind and heart. And the peace I give is a gift the world cannot give. So don't be troubled or afraid." (John 14:27)

———•———

Let's pray…

Father, even when things are not as I would have hoped for or expected, I choose to give you my life. I choose to submit to your will for my life, not my own. Father, these are my worries (be specific) *and these are my needs* (list them). *Father, I thank you for your faithfulness and kindness towards me. Thank you for…* (again, be specific and thank the Father for three things to begin with. If it's too tricky to think of any don't panic. How about thanking God for the gift of breath that you have, the ability to read His Word, the gift of the Holy Spirit). *Holy Spirit, I invite you to overshadow me and fill me completely that I would know a deep and certain peace that surpasses understanding. Amen.*

DAY 15:
SHIPWRECKS

*"When the storms of life come, the wicked are whirled away, but
the godly have a lasting foundation."*
(Proverbs 10:25)

In Acts 27 we read the dramatic account of Paul's journeys, written by his travel companion Luke. Whilst under arrest, Paul set sail towards Rome where he was to appear on trial.

"Putting out to sea from there, we encountered strong headwinds that made it difficult to keep the ship on course, so we sailed north of Cyprus between the island and the mainland ... We had several days of slow sailing, and after great difficulty we finally neared Cnidus. But the wind was against us, ... We struggled along the coast with great difficulty and finally arrived at Fair Havens, near the town of Lasea. We had lost a lot of time. The weather was becoming dangerous for sea travel because it was so late in the fall, and Paul spoke to the ship's officers about it. 'Men,' he said, 'I believe there is trouble ahead if we go on—shipwreck, loss of cargo, and danger to our lives as well.' But the officer in charge of the prisoners listened more to the ship's captain and the owner

than to Paul." (Acts 27:4; 27:7-11)

The ship's officer was a man on a mission. He had a job to do, deadlines to meet, pressures to respond to concerning his cargo of both people and goods. Understandably, perhaps, he listened to his captain rather than the voice of godly wisdom. Choosing whose voice we listen to is a key factor in being victorious when travelling through life's storms.

Now consider Paul. The Lord had a purpose for Paul's life, which included getting him to Rome to stand trial. Of all the things that Paul was required to surrender to the Lord during his life, this trial seems particularly harsh. He wasn't taking a pleasure cruise, he was on his way to stand trial. But he might just lose his life before then, if the crew didn't listen to him!

Paul saw beyond his human trial and knew God always has a bigger plan. God's greater plan would enable him to take the gospel to new territories, to speak into untouched hearts and declare the truth about Jesus. Paul embraced the adventure with Christ, knowing that it was about more than his daily experiences, it was ultimately about God's glory.

In the storm the Lord encouraged Paul and because he took God as His word he was able to encourage others. Paul did not question or doubt. He just trusted what God had said.

"The next day, as gale-force winds continued to batter the ship, the crew began throwing the cargo overboard. The following day they even took some of the ship's gear and threw it overboard. The terrible storm raged for many days, blotting out the sun and the stars, until at last all hope was gone. No one had eaten for a long time. Finally, Paul called the crew together and said, 'Men, you should have listened to me in the first place and not left Crete. You would have avoided all this damage and loss. But take courage! None of you will lose your lives, even though the ship will go down.

For last night an angel of the God to whom I belong and whom I serve stood beside me, and he said, "Don't be afraid, Paul, for you will surely stand trial before Caesar! What's more, God in his goodness has granted safety to everyone sailing with you." So take courage! For I believe God. It will be just as he said. But we will be shipwrecked on an island." (Acts 27:18-25)

I cannot imagine the full terror that the passengers on this ship must have experienced as they plunged into the water, swimming if they were able, or clinging on to broken boat-debris; the salty water burning their throats as they gasped to breathe and keep their heads above the waves. Yet, as promised, the Lord got them all to shore and onto solid ground. Once they have recovered they would need to get a new boat and head back out onto the waters.

After passing through the storm of cancer, I recall my husband cheerily telling me that whilst we had made it, we travelled on stormy seas, so we shouldn't think that we would never face another storm. It wasn't what I wanted to hear right then, but we were driving somewhere in the car, so I couldn't escape his wisdom at that precise moment! Of course, he was right – there would be other storms.

Storms come to us, and we pass through them. But they can be part of our story of victory, rather than defeat. Paul sought the Lord in his storm and was able to say, *"Take courage, for I believe God"* (Acts 27:25). So can we.

Today, let us lean into the Lord for victory and, in spite of the storms, believe God. When I passed through the storm of cancer Psalm 18 became a daily point of focus for me. The drama in this Psalm is as powerful as when Luke talks of the shipwreck. I encourage you to take time to read the whole Psalm and understand God's desire to rescue you.

It is written:

"I love you, Lord; you are my strength. The Lord is my rock, my fortress, and my saviour; my God is my rock, in whom I find protection. He is my shield, the power that saves me, and my place of safety. I called on the Lord, who is worthy of praise, and he saved me from my enemies. The ropes of death entangled me; floods of destruction swept over me. The grave wrapped its ropes around me; death laid a trap in my path. But in my distress I cried out to the Lord; yes, I prayed to my God for help. He heard me from his sanctuary; my cry to him reached his ears." (Psalm 18:1-6)

Let's pray...

Lord, I love you and thank you that you do not keep your distance, but you hear my cry and come and rescue me. Lord, in this storm (be specific) *may I hear you speak, rescue and save me. Lord, bring me to a place of safety. Amen.*

DAY 16:
SHAKE IT OFF

"Like a fluttering sparrow or a darting swallow, an undeserved curse will not land on its intended victim."
(Proverbs 26:2)

Jesus was tempted by the enemy to throw Himself off the highest point in the city, as that wouldn't have hurt Him. As a human, however, clearly it would have. Stuff happens in life that really hurts and can damage us. It is inevitable. What helped Jesus get through His challenges? He wasn't simply considering His current circumstances, He was aware of what His future held.

It helps us to cope with some of the troubles we face in life if we have an eternal perspective. There is comfort to be had in knowing that our ultimate future is safe in God's hands; that there will come a point where no more harm can come to us. But in the meantime, doesn't it seem that we can be surrounded by insecurity; unprotected from harm?

In Acts 28, having survived the shipwreck as the Lord promised, Paul arrived on the island of Malta. The people were friendly so the survivors received a warm welcome. Since they had dragged themselves out of the sea, and it was cold and raining, the island's inhabitants built a fire to warm Paul and his colleagues. We read how, as Paul helped gather wood for the fire, a poisonous snake driven out by the heat, launched out and bit him on the hand. The dramatic account says that, *"the people of the island saw it hanging from his hand"* (Acts 28:3). The locals assumed that Paul must be a murderer who was experiencing "justice". However, *"Paul shook off the snake into the fire and was unharmed"* (Acts 28:5)

Some things do not have to be endured. Some things can be shaken off.

I heard a funny story once about a donkey. The donkey fell into a well and was well and truly stuck. The farmer who owned it wasn't that bothered by this turn of events. He didn't much like this old donkey and was glad it was out of his way. So the farmer decided to bury the donkey in the well and called some neighbours to help him. Grabbing spades they started to shovel mud and throw it down the well. The little donkey did not like the mud raining down on him in the well and every time some fell onto his back he shook it off. The mud gathered around his feet and so he stepped up onto it. Mud kept falling, shovel by shovel, and the donkey kept shaking it off and stepping up. Eventually, after a lot of shovelling and a lot of shaking-it-off and stepping-up, the donkey reached the top of the well. Looking the farmer square in the eye, he shook himself off and stepped out.

There are some things that the enemy would like to attach to us, or bury us under. But our response can be to shake it off and step up.

Paul shook off the snake that grabbed hold of his hand. It fell into the fire and was burned up. The story in Acts continues...

"Near the shore where we landed was an estate belonging to Publius, the chief official of the island. He welcomed us and treated us kindly for three days. As it happened, Publius's father was ill with

fever and dysentery. Paul went in and prayed for him, and laying his hands on him, he healed him. Then all the other sick people on the island came and were healed. As a result we were showered with honours, and when the time came to sail, people supplied us with everything we would need for the trip." (Acts 28:7-10)

The hands that could have been in agony, filled with poison, were the hands that God used to reach out and minister healing to those in need. Suddenly, the same people who suspected Paul must be a murderer, were honouring him and supplying provisions for the rest of his journey. Paul shook it off and stepped up.

Paul wrote to the Romans saying,

"What shall we say about such wonderful things as these? If God is for us, who can ever be against us? Since he did not spare even his own Son but gave him up for us all, won't he also give us everything else? Who dares accuse us whom God has chosen for his own? No one—for God himself has given us right standing with himself. Who then will condemn us? No one—for Christ Jesus died for us and was raised to life for us, and he is sitting in the place of honour at God's right hand, pleading for us." (Romans 8:31-34)

We can shake it off and step up because Jesus Christ suffered and endured for us, and is now sitting up! Jesus is sitting at the right hand of the Father, pleading for us. Because of this we can be confident that all things are going to work for our good. We will be victorious against every scheme of the enemy.

Today, consider what you need to shake off and step up from. Are there challenges at home, in your community or workplace, that can be shaken off and stepped up from? What the enemy seeks for evil can be turned around for the glory of the Lord in your life.

It is written:

"But in that coming day no weapon turned against you will

succeed. You will silence every voice   raised up to accuse you. These benefits are enjoyed by the servants of the Lord; their vindication will come from me. I, the Lord, have spoken!" (Isaiah 54:17)

———•———

Let's pray...

Lord, I thank you that even if weapons are formed against me they will not prosper because you have said so, and you are praying for me right now. Today, Lord, I choose to walk through this day following you closely. Please silence every voice that is raised in accusation against me and help me shake off any attempt from the enemy to weigh me down. Amen.

DAY 17:
MADE IN THE IMAGE

"An honest witness tells the truth; a false witness tells lies."
(Proverbs 12:17)

Do you remember the dot-to-dot pictures you may have done as a child, when your wriggly lines followed a sequence of numbers until a picture was revealed? The more numbers there were, the more intricate the final picture would be. For me, rushing the process meant that I would often assume where the next number should be and rush off in the wrong direction!

As we grow in victory with the word of God we find there is a spiritual "joining of the dots" that happens. We begin to get a much clearer picture of the Father's deep love for us and the enemy's constant scheming to undermine it.

Some time ago a friend helped me join a few dots together and it really helped me. So today I want to join the dots in a way you might not have seen before. Keep following the numbers – the picture will come together.

In the book of Acts we read about Peter having a vision from the Lord where he saw the sky open and a large sheet of cloth lowered before him containing all types of animals. The invitation came from heaven to "come and eat". To Peter, a Jewish man, the food on offer was "unclean" and he therefore rejected the invitation. The vision-invitation was repeated three times, however – a sure sign that the Lord wanted to communicate an important message. Through persistent repetition the Lord said,

"Do not call something unclean if God has made it clean." (Acts 10:15)

This revelation led to Peter's obedient response of sharing the gospel with the Gentile Cornelius and so the gospel went beyond the Jewish community.

There is an important principle here, beyond the fact of understanding the Father's heart for the spread of His love. We must not be a people who call unclean something that has been made clean. Time and time again the enemy will trap us in declaring ourselves "unclean". What do I mean? Let's consider body image!

Many of us look in the mirror as if we're looking at one of those distorted fair ground mirrors. We grimace and declare that we are too fat, too skinny, too short, too tall, too hairy, too hair-free, too pale, too dark, too ugly ... and so on. But as we do this, we are calling bad something that God has called good. We are calling unclean, that which God longs to call clean.

We compare ourselves to the visual images displayed all around. Images wallpaper our world, but most have been airbrushed and edited. We take them at face value, but actually they are unreal. Instead of comparing ourselves to this false reality, the Lord wants to assure us that,

"God created human beings in his own image (surely He is not ugly. The only ugliness associate with the Lord is the ugliness of Jesus' death on the cross. He became ugly with our sin in order to make us clean) *In the image of God he created them; male and*

female he created them … God looked over all he had made and he saw that it was very good!" (Genesis 1:27,31)

Just as Jesus was tempted to throw Himself down, so we are all too easily persuaded to throw ourselves into a pit of self-loathing, effectively calling the Lord a liar! We call bad what He has called "very good".

At the age of 8 I was diagnosed with a pigmentation disease called Vitiligo. One particular hospital appointment is etched in my memory, when my entire body was examined to determine the extent of the white patches on my skin. My parents were close to hand, but nonetheless I felt vulnerable, exposed and, to be honest, something of a freak. The pigmentation issue is really not too severe in my case and mostly occurs in places that are not on public display. Yet the enemy has used this to cause me to be unappreciative of how God has created me. It takes active choice to be a witness for God's truth and not align with the enemy's lies.

Consider how you were crafted – intentionally and wonderfully – and how you are known in every way, as David writes in Psalm 139:

"O Lord, you have examined my heart and know everything about me. You know when I sit down or stand up. You know my thoughts even when I'm far away. You see me when I travel and when I rest at home. You know everything I do. You know what I am going to say even before I say it, Lord. You go before me and follow me. You place your hand of blessing on my head. Such knowledge is too wonderful for me, too great for me to understand! … You made all the delicate, inner parts of my body and knit me together in my mother's womb. Thank you for making me so wonderfully complex! Your workmanship is marvellous—how well I know it. You watched me as I was being formed in utter seclusion, as I was woven together in the dark of the womb. You saw me before I was

born. *Every day of my life was recorded in your book. Every moment was laid out before a single day had passed. How precious are your thoughts about me, O God. They cannot be numbered! I can't even count them; they outnumber the grains of sand! And when I wake up, you are still with me!"* (Psalm 139:1-5,13-18)

Today, as you look in the mirror, instead of dismissing or even calling ugly what the Lord calls "very good", wield your sword in the face of the enemy's taunts and declare with thanks to your Creator, as it is written,

"...thank you for making me so wonderfully complex! Your workmanship is marvellous." (Psalm 139:14)

——·——

Let's pray...

Father, I am sorry for declaring what you have called clean, unclean. I am sorry that I've seen myself in a distorted way and believed the enemy's lies. Please forgive me. Thank you, Jesus, that you became ugly for me so that I could be made right with God. Thank you that I am fearfully and wonderfully made. Thank you that all of my complexities and uniqueness are part of your beautiful plan because you made me in your image. Amen.

DAY 18:
GIANTS AND GRASSHOPPERS

"When people's lives please the Lord, even their enemies are at peace with them."
(Proverbs 16:7)

As we continue our forty day journey to discover and grow in victory we're going to consider another journey that a group of explorers took many years ago: twelve men, sent out on a wilderness journey to explore a new land that was a land full of promise, yet full of challenge.

Moses sent out twelve leaders from the tribes of Israel to explore the promised land of Canaan. All the men came back taken by the fertility and fruitfulness of the land, but ten were overwhelmed by the size of the inhabitants, who appeared to them like giants, making them feel like "grasshoppers" by comparison. In stark contrast, two of the twelve men saw the challenges but understood that their God was bigger. Caleb and Joshua implored the people to press ahead:

"They said to all the people of Israel, 'The land we travelled through and explored is a wonderful land! And if the Lord is pleased with us, he will bring us safely into that land and give it to us. It is

a rich land flowing with milk and honey. Do not rebel against the Lord, and don't be afraid of the people of the land. They are only helpless prey to us! They have no protection, but the Lord is with us! Don't be afraid of them!" (Numbers 14:7-9)

You might have heard it said before that we would be wise to stop telling the Lord how big our problems are and instead start telling our problems how big our God is. Caleb and Joshua understood that however big their enemies were, their God was even bigger.

Now, admittedly, I haven't often likened myself to a grasshopper, but I have found myself feeling insignificant and smaller than the challenges I've had to face; feeling unqualified, incompetent or unworthy to meet them. If we focus on our challenges then we may well feel like the ten explorers who were intimidated, besieged by grasshopper mentality. However, victory comes when we take our eyes off our own inadequacy and look to God who is the source of our help. And who, frankly, is more than adequate!

By focussing on the hugeness of the opposition we can be left paralysed by fear and choose no-action rather than steps of obedience; avoiding the challenge rather than pressing on and allowing the Lord to do what He wants to do.

Paul wrote to the believers of Corinth encouraging them that their weaknesses were the point at which God could meet them and reveal His strength and glory the most. He recalled that the Lord had said to him, *"My grace is all you need. My power works best in weakness."* Paul concluded that, *"Now I am glad to boast about my weaknesses, so that the power of Christ can work through me. That's why I take pleasure in my weaknesses, and in the insults, hardships, persecutions, and troubles I suffer for Christ. For when I am weak, then I am strong."* (2 Corinthians 12:8-10)

One time I was preaching "the triple" in our home church

(two services in the morning and one in the afternoon) and in between service two and three my husband and I were engaged in a conversation with someone that caught me a little off guard. I thought I knew what this person wanted to chat about, but in fact there was an additional agenda – one that left me feeling personally attacked, insulted and vulnerable. I responded as graciously as I could at the time, but as I walked away from the conversation and headed into the next service I felt devastated.

I can't imagine feeling more like a crushed grasshopper than I did then. My heart was breaking as service began and we entered into a time of praise. Two minutes before I was due to preach my heart was heavy and I leaned into Tim and confessed that I didn't think I would be able to preach. I didn't want to press on. I felt so vulnerable and couldn't hold back a few tears. As I spoke to Tim, wounded, wanting him to rescue me, he lovingly (and wisely) told me to depend on the Lord; to simply open my mouth and let the Father say what He wanted to say. Yet again, I was reminded that God is way bigger than my weakness. Not only did I manage to speak without crying, but there was an anointing of humour on the message which had not been in the previous services. People in the room were able to hear from God. He was so gracious and spoke so powerfully and clearly through me. The sermon was great, not because I was great – I was a human-grasshopper! – but because God loves taking my weakness and showing His greater strength and grace through me.

I don't like being caught off guard and insulted by unkind and unhelpful words, but if it means that my words become God's words as I preach, then for the sake of His gospel, as Paul said, so be it. The wounds can be healed by the same God who shows His strength through my weakness.

"I look up to the mountains— does my help come from there?

My help comes from the Lord, who made heaven and earth! He will not let you stumble; the one who watches over you will not slumber. Indeed, he who watches over Israel never slumbers or sleeps. The Lord himself watches over you!" (Psalm 121:1-5)

David was tempted to be overwhelmed and throw himself down, yet he knew to lift his eyes heavenward. Today, look above the mountain of challenge that is in front of you and instead look to the one who is bigger than any challenge. Look to the Lord. He is your help. It really doesn't matter how small we feel and how big the challenge is when we are walking in obedience and faith with the Lord.

It is written:

"The Lord keeps you from all harm and watches over your life. The Lord keeps watch over you as you come and go, both now and forever." (Psalm 121:7-8)

———•———

Let's pray...

Lord, today may I see how big you are in comparison to any challenges, troubles and battles that I might face. I choose to lift my eyes above my circumstances and look to you, my true help. Thank you that you are keeping watch over me as I come and go throughout my day today. Lord, I love you and I trust your strength and protection. Amen.

DAY 19:
WORD OF PROMISE

———•———

"Truthful words stand the test of time, but lies are soon exposed."
(Proverbs 12:19)

Two small children stand whispering together, making an agreement. Their promises to each other sealed by entwining their little fingers in a pinkie-promise. How long does the childish promise hold, once their fingers are untwined and they've walked away? A few years later and the grown kids are sealing their promises with, "I swear I'll do it!" And they mean it … for a while. But our intentions are often overcome in the course of time and promises undone.

Have you ever been frustrated by people who say one thing but do another? Unfulfilled promises in others can be exasperating. Then there is the shame we can feel if we have to break our own promises and let others down.

The apostle James addresses this issue, writing to Christ's followers, *"But most of all, my brothers and sisters, never take an oath, by heaven or earth or anything else. Just say a simple yes or no, so that you will not sin and be condemned."* (James 5:12)

James was no doubt echoing the words of Jesus, who told a parable about a father who was trying to get his two sons to help him in his vineyard. The older son says he won't help, but later changes his mind and blesses his father by choosing to help in the end, choosing to be obedient. The younger son says that he will help, but then doesn't follow through on his pledge, taking the path of disobedience.

If we're honest, all of us have let someone down at one time or another, just as we have been let down by others. Following Jesus closely will enable us to become more and more like Him, which means we won't be promise-breakers. However, it doesn't guarantee that we won't be on the receiving end of other peoples' broken promises.

With regard to God's promises, this can sometimes be a mental battleground for us. We sometimes try to understand Father God by our own human standards. It often seems to us that God is slow in fulfilling His promises, but we need to trust that He knows best. During these waiting times the word of God offers us reassurance. In the book of Numbers, the prophet Balaam speaking to Balak makes this very point:

"God is not a man, so he does not lie. He is not human, so he does not change his mind. Has he ever spoken and failed to act? Has he ever promised and not carried it through? Listen, I received a command to bless; God has blessed, and I cannot reverse it!" (Numbers 23:19-20)

It was Moses who heard the initial promise of God regarding the Promised Land. It referred to the entire nation of Israel, but surely Moses was an intended recipient of the promise. In the end, though, he wasn't. Not because God had changed his mind, but because Moses tragically disqualified himself when he didn't fully believe that the Lord would fulfil His word and provide water from the rock. So we read these heart rending words:

"One day the Lord said to Moses, 'Climb one of the mountains east of the river, and look out over the land I have given the people of Israel. After you have seen it, you will die like your brother, Aaron, for you both rebelled against my instructions in the wilderness of Zin. When the people of Israel rebelled, you failed to demonstrate my holiness to them at the waters.'" (Numbers 27:12-14)

Even in the wilderness the Lord expected Moses to be obedient, but instead of following the Lord's instructions he took matters into his own hands. Doesn't it make your heart sink for Moses to get so far, but not all the way?

So God raises up Joshua as his successor. Full of faith, with his eyes focussed firmly on the greatness of God, Joshua realised that when God speaks He always delivers. Even though he'd seen the great leader, Moses, fall at the penultimate hurdle, Joshua remained assured in the unchangeable God, solid as a rock:

"Deep in your hearts you know that every promise of the Lord your God has come true. Not a single one has failed! But as surely as the Lord your God has given you the good things he promised, he will also bring disaster on you if you disobey him. He will completely destroy you from this good land he has given you. If you break the covenant of the Lord your God by worshiping and serving other gods, his anger will burn against you, and you will quickly vanish from the good land he has given you." (Joshua 23:14-16)

Our God is a holy, righteous God, so we must not be complacent. But by trusting His incredible promises we, like Joshua, can be confident that He is an awesome God and a good Father. God is unchanging. We can have great confidence in His absolute consistency. Even when all else seems to shift and change around us, He does not.

Today, let us give thanks to God that He will never, ever break

His promises to us. Are there some promises that the Lord has spoken to you that have not yet come to pass? Is He desiring more of your fellowship, intimacy and obedience that He might show His love for you more clearly?

For it is written,

"Whatever is good and perfect is a gift coming down to us from God our Father, who created all the lights in the heavens. He never changes or casts a shifting shadow. He chose to give birth to us by giving us his true word. And we, out of all creation, became his prized possession." (James 1:17-18)

Let's pray...

Lord, I thank you for your favour and your mercy and your faithfulness to your children over all the years. I thank you that you do not, and will not, break your promises. Today Lord, may my yes to you be a true yes! May I be obedient and follow through on what I promise to do for you. Thank you that I am one of your prized possessions. Amen.

DAY 20:
SHORT TERM MEMORY LOSS

"For whoever finds me finds life and receives favour from the
Lord."
(Proverbs 8: 35)

Every Monday the staff team of our church gather together to start the week sharing a time of worship and encouraging one another in the word of God. It's a wonderful way to start the week. Each staff member takes it in turn to lead the devotions and on one such occasion we were led into a conversation about short term memory loss. Not in the medical sense but in the spiritual! In Mark's gospel we read the time when Jesus seemed to be frustrated by the short term memory loss of His disciples. They'd seen Him miraculously feed five thousand people before miraculously feeding another four thousand people – then they got into this discussion.

"At this they began to argue with each other because they hadn't brought any bread. Jesus knew what they were saying, so he said, 'Why are you arguing about having no bread? Don't you know or understand even yet? Are your hearts too hard to take it in? "You have eyes—can't you see? You have ears—can't you hear?" Don't

you remember anything at all? When I fed the 5,000 with five loaves of bread, how many baskets of leftovers did you pick up afterward?' 'Twelve,' they said. 'And when I fed the 4,000 with seven loaves, how many large baskets of leftovers did you pick up?' 'Seven,' they said. 'Don't you understand yet?' he asked them."* (Mark 8:16-21)

The very next story that Mark writes about is the healing of a blind man – surely making the point that whilst the disciples had eyes they were clearly not seeing well. The disciples were forgetting what they had seen before.

It's easy to point to the disciples and do a little tutting. How forgetful were they? They lived with Jesus, up close and personal, surely they were well aware of the miracles they saw every day?

The truth is, we frequently suffer with the same spiritual short-term memory loss – forgetting what Jesus has already done for us.

In the wilderness, when Jesus was tempted to throw Himself from the highest point of the city, He responded by saying, *"You must not test the Lord your God"* (Deuteronomy 6:16). The verses surrounding that phrase from Deuteronomy give us a bigger perspective on what Jesus was saying:

"Be careful not to forget the Lord, who rescued you from slavery in the land of Egypt. You must fear the Lord your God and serve him. When you take an oath, you must use only his name. You must not worship any of the gods of neighbouring nations, for the Lord your God, who lives among you, is a jealous God. His anger will flare up against you, and he will wipe you from the face of the earth. You must not test the Lord your God as you did when you complained at Massah. You must diligently obey the commands of the Lord your God—all the laws and decrees he has given you. Do what is right and good in the Lord's sight, so all will go well with you. Then you will enter and occupy the good land that the Lord swore to give your ancestors. You will drive out all

the enemies living in the land, just as the Lord said you would."
(Deuteronomy 6:12-19)

The enemy was familiar with Scripture. This one small sentence reminded him not only of God's people being liberated from captivity, but also the fact that – like all God's enemies – he would in time be "driven from the land". I can imagine a few eaves dropping angels high-fiving each other as Jesus brought this weighty reminder.

Deuteronomy was written to record the covenant between God and the people of Israel – to help the followers of God remember, for the sake of future generations, not just where they were from but where they were heading. It also served as a reminder that the people should continue looking to God and worshipping Him only, if they were to benefit from His favour.

Obedience can feel uncomfortable (remember our discussion about self-discipline), but is necessary for our growth and maturity in Christ. We may prefer to skip some parts of our journey, but God wants us to persevere in trusting Him. Jesus knew His mission on earth. He knew that He would have to face the Garden of Gethsemane and the cross in order to see His Father's will accomplished. He would have liked to, but knew He couldn't, bypass the pain of His humanity. Jesus fell back on His experience of the Father. He chose to remember His Father's character, His goodness, and trust Him to the end.

Today, as we consider the favour that we would like to enjoy from the Lord, let's think about the obedience that we will offer Him. Let's remember what He has done for us over the years; how He has revealed His goodness to us. Let us use our eyes to see the work of the Lord and choose to take courage form this. It is written:

"Do what is right and good in the Lord's sight, so all will go well with you." (Deuteronomy 6:18)

———•———

Let's pray…

Father, please help me remember your favour and your goodness; help me to focus on our shared experiences over the years. Please help me to not forget. Thank you for your favour. Lord, help me to remember to do what is right by you today. Amen.

DAY 21:
IT'S NOT MY FAULT

"People who conceal their sins will not prosper, but if they confess and turn from them, they will receive mercy."
(Proverbs 28:13)

I love being the mother of three most incredible children. I love how they can all come from the same family line and yet be so different. However, one thing I've observed is that they've all been able to learn and use one phrase – a phrase that they will recite with passion – the infamous, "It's not my fault!" It sometimes seems as though they will go to any lengths to blame, quite frankly, anyone else in the midst of a dispute and as means of expunging all consequences for themselves.

As a fallible parent, I'm sure there have been times when my wisdom was lacking, and I held the wrong person responsible for some misdemeanour. This can be frustrating and hurtful for the innocent party (though many a parent would say there are rarely any totally "innocent" parties). In such situations, I try to apply the same godly wisdom that Solomon had an abundance of – *"wisdom that God had given him for rendering justice"* (1 Kings 3:28) – so that I too don't damage any babies!

From the very beginning mankind picked up the bad habit of covering their wrong actions and hiding behind a disclaimer of "no-responsibility". It was Adam and Eve's response when the Lord challenged them about eating the forbidden fruit? Adam immediately blamed the woman and the woman immediately blamed the serpent, swiftly passing the responsibility for the situation on to the deceiver, rather than the deceived. Since then, humanity has always been looking for someone else to blame. God is blamed for so much stuff that happens in our fallen world: death, sickness, famine, earthquakes!

The subtle deception of the enemy in the Garden, "Did God really say?", echoed down the centuries as Jesus was tempted with, "If you *are* the Son of God…". The enemy's tactic has not changed; he still wants to trap us into blame shifting and abdicating our responsibilities; sowing seeds of doubt so that we will blame someone else for the things that go wrong in our lives, ideally God.

When we are tempted to blame God for something bad that is happening in our lives, we must focus again on His unchanging character and His desire to do good to us. His heart towards us is only love. If He does allow (not send) adverse circumstances in our lives, it is for the greater cause of forming Christ in us and growing us spiritually. God only gives good gifts. Trials will prove our faith and display His glory through us. Sometimes pruning is needed for greater fruitfulness in the future as the Lord refines us. Blaming God for the bad things only serves to camouflage our enemy. It is time to recognise the battle we're in, realise that our enemy is real, and commit to trusting in Jesus, come what may. As Jesus taught His disciples:

"I am the true grapevine, and my Father is the gardener. He cuts off every branch of mine that doesn't produce fruit, and he prunes

the branches that do bear fruit so they will produce even more. You have already been pruned and purified by the message I have given you. Remain in me, and I will remain in you. For a branch cannot produce fruit if it is severed from the vine, and you cannot be fruitful unless you remain in me. Yes, I am the vine; you are the branches. Those who remain in me, and I in them, will produce much fruit. For apart from me you can do nothing. Anyone who does not remain in me is thrown away like a useless branch and withers. Such branches are gathered into a pile to be burned. But if you remain in me and my words remain in you, you may ask for anything you want, and it will be granted! When you produce much fruit, you are my true disciples. This brings great glory to my Father." (John 15:1-8)

Pruning can be uncomfortable, painful and disturbing, but it's for our good. To enable us to produce much more fruit there might be some essential pruning.

Consider whether, perhaps, sinful choices have led to some current harsh circumstances in your life. If so, deal with this swiftly by confessing to the Lord and allowing Him to bring restoration. We know that, *"If we confess our sins to him, he is faithful and just to forgive us our sins and to cleanse us from all wickedness"* (1 John 1:9). But let's not blame anyone else for that which is our responsibility.

Today, focus on all the good things that God has done in your life. Remember again the love of the Father. It is written:

"For the Lord is good. His unfailing love continues forever, and his faithfulness continues to each generation." (Psalm 100:5)

———•———

Let's pray...

Father, I thank you for the wisdom you give us if we ask. Please give me the wisdom and grace to take responsibility for my actions without shifting blame to others. Give me the wisdom to know when you are doing pruning work in my life and help me to cooperate with you. Thank you that you are for me, have good things for me, and forgive all my sins when I confess them to you. Amen.

DAY 22:
IN THE HIDDEN PLACE

"The seeds of good deeds become a tree of life; a wise person wins friends."
(Proverbs 11:30)

During the years when we were trying to conceive our second child I went through various phantom pregnancies. Not in the truest, medical sense, but in the I'm-late-so-surely-I-must-be wishful thinking sense. Having an irregular cycle regularly gave me the opportunity to think that I might be pregnant. After buying numerous pregnancy tests, however, my hopes were dashed with some regularity. However much I wanted this miracle to take place, it wasn't happening. Until, of course, the time when it did. Have you ever waited for ages until one day that "suddenly" from God came along?

Finding out I was pregnant with my second child was one of those incredible "suddenlies". From that moment on I entered into the next stage of my faith journey of expectancy. Initially I didn't look pregnant, but I was pregnant. A child was beginning to take shape in the secret place within me, as cells multiplied and the miracle of life grew. Delivering a healthy baby necessitated my journeying the full term of the pregnancy. However keen I was to hold my baby in my arms, I would have to hold it within me first.

So many of the incredible things God does in us start in the "secret place". We might have a hint of what is going on, but it is largely unseen. Furthermore, these hidden happenings can't be hurried. However much we want to hold the fruit of them in our hands, see it with our own eyes, it has to be formed in the hidden place first.

A friend of ours once challenged Tim and I that our vision was too small and our timeline was too short. We wanted things to be delivered now, but God was more interested in some hidden-season-growth that would bring about an even greater harvest.

Many of Jesus' parables were about farmers or gardeners. He spoke about spiritual life in terms of seeds: *"The Kingdom of God is like a farmer who scatters seed on the ground. Night and day, while he's asleep or awake, the seed sprouts and grows, but he does not understand how it happens. The earth produces the crops on its own. First a leaf blade pushes through, then the heads of wheat are formed, and finally the grain ripens. And as soon as the grain is ready, the farmer comes and harvests it with a sickle, for the harvest time has come."* (Mark 4:26-29)

The seeds were hidden in the secret place, but they were destined to grow. Growth was their destiny because of the potential encapsulated within. Night and day growth would happen in the secret place until suddenly shoots appeared on the surface.

Just as Jesus was tempted to shortcut God's purposes, we are tempted to "rush" God's fruit. We get impatient, but the fruit will not come at the expense of a season of growth.

Jesus alluded to this in His parable about seed falling on different terrains: *"Other seed fell on shallow soil with underlying* rock. *The seed sprouted quickly because the soil was shallow. But the plant soon wilted under the hot sun, and since it didn't have deep roots, it died."* (Mark 4:5-6)

Bountiful plants need deep roots. God's passionate commitment to our fruitfulness calls for us to have deep roots in His strong soil.

Isaiah spoke about this same principle to the scattered people of God who were regrouping as a remnant of believers: *"You who are left in Judah, who have escaped the ravages of the siege, will put roots down in your own soil and will grow up and flourish. For a remnant of my people will spread out from Jerusalem, a group of survivors from Mount Zion. The passionate commitment of the Lord of Heaven's Armies will make this happen!"* (2 Kings 19:30-31)

I was praying with a couple of friends recently who had been going through an incredibly hard time, and whose marriage was under serious threat. Whilst praying I became increasingly aware that this precious marriage was under significant attack from the enemy. He was aware of the potential fruit encapsulated within them. I asked a few of our other intercessor friends to begin praying for them. As we did, we saw their marriage begin to turn around. As this precious couple allowed their roots to go down deeper in the hidden place, leaning on Christ as much as they were able, and encouraging each other, so the shoots of life began to show.

Just as the enemy knew that Jesus' destiny was of enormous significance, he also understands that our destiny in Christ is significant. The fruit of a life submitted to Christ is great, so the enemy will want to undermine us before we begin to bear that fruit.

Today, recognise any root-work of a hidden season and allow your roots to go down deep by growing in the word, growing in relationships which encourage you, and allow the soil of the local church to nourish you. It is this connection with Christ Himself that leads to a truly fruitful life.

It is written:

"Yes, I am the vine; you are the branches. Those who remain in me, and I in them, will produce much fruit. For apart from me you can do nothing. Anyone who does not remain in me is thrown away like a useless branch and withers. Such branches are gathered into a pile to be burned. But if you remain in me and my words remain in you, you may ask for anything you want, and it will be granted! When you produce much fruit, you are my true disciples. This brings great glory to my Father." (John 15:5-8)

Let's pray...

Lord, will you help me to not rush the season of growth that you want to do in the hidden place. Please cause my roots to go down deep into healthy soil, so that in your time my life will produce a harvest of fruit for your glory. Amen.

DAY 23:
THE COMING OF AGE

"The glory of the young is their strength; the grey hair of experience is the splendour of the old."
(Proverbs 20:29)

In the book of Job we see the results of a godly man being tested, permitted by the Lord, to prove that even in the face of great temptation it is possible not to sin. Job goes through many battles, and does so in the company of some ill-advised friends who grapple with trying to understand why he is going through them. They leap to wrong assumptions and conclusions.

One of Job's friends, Elihu, tries to understand the tension of wisdom not necessarily going hand in hand with physical maturity. He says, *"I thought, 'Those who are older should speak, for wisdom with age.' But there is a spirit within people, the breath of the Almighty within them, that makes them intelligent. Sometimes the elders are not wise. Sometimes the aged do not understand justice."* (Job 32:6-9). Elihu realised that wisdom doesn't come with age, rather it comes by the Spirit of God within. As far as God is concerned, our age does not qualify or disqualify us.

Paul wrote to Timothy, a leader younger than himself, urging him to, *"Teach these things and insist that everyone learn them. Don't let anyone think less of you because you are young. Be an example to all believers in what you say, in the way you live, in your love, your faith, and your purity. Until I get there, focus on reading the Scriptures to the church, encouraging the believers, and teaching them"* (1 Timothy 4:11-13).

Paul wanted Timothy to understand that biological years don't matter as much as being filled with the Spirit and rooted in the word of God, when it comes to wisdom and leadership.

God is not limited by age, neither is He limited by time. Some would say He dwells outside of time, but actually He is its creator and is simply never constrained by it. We should not, therefore, limit what God can do in our lives on the basis of time.

There was a significant amount of time when the enemy was telling me that I was running out of time! Strangely, not at the time when I was dealing with a life-threatening illness, but when my dream of having children was not becoming a reality and successive birthdays came and went. The enemy kept on telling me that I was getting older – I should give up on my dreams, because I would never see them come to pass.

Can you see the trap? These lies not only rob us of hope for the future, but they make us complicit as we give up making any effort to trust God for our dreams. Paul said that we are co-workers with the Lord to see His purposes fulfilled (1 Corinthians 3:9 NIV), revealing a role for us in active participation in the purposes of the Lord.

In Genesis we read the wonderful story of Abraham, the father of faith, and his wife Sarah being visited by the Lord and told that even in their old age they would have a baby.

"'I will return to you about this time next year, and your wife, Sarah, will have a son!' Sarah was listening to this conversation

from the tent. Abraham and Sarah were both very old by this time, and Sarah was long past the age of having children. So she laughed silently to herself and said, 'How could a worn-out woman like me enjoy such pleasure, especially when my master—my husband—is also so old?' Then the Lord said to Abraham, 'Why did Sarah laugh? Why did she say, "Can an old woman like me have a baby?" Is anything too hard for the Lord? I will return about this time next year, and Sarah will have a son.' Sarah was afraid, so she denied it, saying, 'I didn't laugh.' But the Lord said, 'No, you did laugh.'" (Genesis 18:10-15)

Many assume that Sarah's laugh was full of negative, hardened doubt. I think Sarah laughed because she could hardly dare believe that the Lord would favour her in such a profound way, especially when she discredited herself by her age. Whilst she was fearful of the consequences of any doubt towards the Lord, He, as loving Father, was committed to blessing and furthering His purposes through her.

Today, if the enemy tempts you to throw your dreams down and give up on who you are called to be and what you are called to do, pick up your sword and allow it to be sharpened and at the ready.

It is written: *"Humanly speaking, it is impossible. But with God everything is possible."* (Matthew 19:22)

————•————

Let's pray...

Lord, may my years, whether feeling too few or too many, serve only to display your glory even more. Let my inexperience be what you use to show your glory and grace. Let my many years shout out as testimony to your goodness and your favour. Let my age not limit your purposes. I choose to be your co-worker for your service and for your glory every day. Amen.

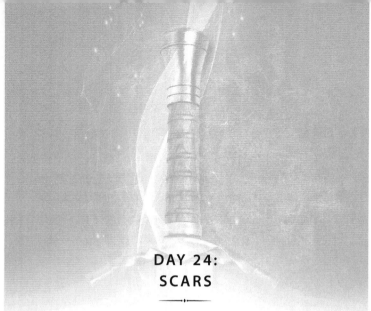

DAY 24:
SCARS

———•———

"Wounds from a sincere friend are better than many kisses from an enemy."
(Proverbs 27:6)

When I was a young child I remember playing on a roundabout with some friends when somehow the centrifugal force came into effect and I was flung off the roundabout, landing with a thud on the surrounding mud. Of course, this entertained my friends a great deal, but I was not amused. In fact, the experience left a mark on me, which I carry to this day. Not a fear of roundabouts, but a tiny scar on my knee from some sharp object that caught me as I landed. Because it happened whilst I was (mostly) having fun, I call it a "happy wound". This is something I've passed on to my children whenever, over the years, a fun game has ended in tears. At least it was a happy wound. In truth, I've sometimes said this to distract them from their tears. So even in play we can pick up injuries and wounds.

Tim and I were chatting with dear friends of ours recently when the subject of scars came up. One of our friends had recently undergone surgery for a hernia. Nearly three months on, the area of the wound, whilst appearing to be healed, was still overly sensitive in places and numb in others. We then had one of those potentially awkward conversations of comparing scars (not in a show-and-tell way, just "tell"!).

The area around a scar can still be sensitive or even slightly numb years after gaining it. Life-wounds that are more emotional than physical can also leave us the same: either overly sensitive or actually numb. How do such wounds occur? They can be caused by unexpected words that are hurtful, by rejection from someone we've loved and trusted, by the loss of a loved one – whether we were expecting it or not – or by a relationship breakdown. Then there are unexpected illnesses, sudden changes in employment status, and seemingly unanswered prayers. This list is not exhaustive, but you get the idea.

Our enemy would like to play on our wounds to keep us over sensitive, numbed by hardened scar tissue and so restricted in our faith. He tells us the lie that we will never be free of the pain. Hopelessness can take root as we settle for and accept a new "normal". But this is not the Father's heart for us! Jesus suffered terrible wounds in order to deal with ours, as Isaiah prophesied in this incredible passage:

"He was despised and rejected— a man of sorrows, acquainted with deepest grief. We turned our backs on him and looked the other way. He was despised, and we did not care. Yet it was our weaknesses he carried; it was our sorrows that weighed him down. And we thought his troubles were a punishment from God, a punishment for his own sins! But he was pierced for our rebellion, crushed for our sins. He was beaten so we could be whole. He was whipped so we could be healed. All of us, like sheep, have strayed away. We have left God's paths to follow our own. Yet the Lord laid on him the sins of us all." (Isaiah 53:3-6)

Our wounds are healed because Jesus was wounded for us. This was no accident. This was no playful game going wrong. This was an elective eternal plan come to fruition – that in His death our wounds, our sins, our sorrow, our pain was all laid on Him. He was wounded so that we can be healed.

Echoing these words, Peter writes in his letter of the sinless Jesus who,

"...committed no sin, and no deceit was found in his mouth. When they hurled their insults at him, he did not retaliate; when he suffered, he made no threats. Instead, he entrusted himself to him who judges justly. 'He himself bore our sins' in his body on the cross, so that we might die to sins and live for righteousness; 'by his wounds you have been healed.' For 'you were like sheep going astray,' but now you have returned to the Shepherd and Overseer of your souls." (1 Peter 2:22-25)

In the days of His resurrection Jesus appeared on numerous occasions to His disciples. *"The doors were locked; but suddenly, as before, Jesus was standing among them. 'Peace be with you,' he said. Then he said to Thomas, 'Put your finger here, and look at my hands. Put your hand into the wound in my side. Don't be faithless any longer. Believe!'"* (John 20:26-27)

Today, the Lord wants to walk into the situations we've locked away. He wants to walk into our pain, our hurts, our fears, our disbeliefs. We can be like Thomas and reach out to Jesus and experience His wounds, knowing that He has dealt with ours for all time.

As Ezekiel wrote of the Lord's healing: *"I will give you a new heart, and I will put a new spirit in you. I will take out your stony, stubborn heart and give you a tender, responsive heart."* (Ezekiel 36:26)

It is written:

"O Lord, if you heal me, I will be truly healed; if you save me, I will be truly saved. My praises are for you alone!" (Jeremiah 17:14)

Let's pray...

O Lord, I will bring my praise to you alone. Only in you is my true healing. Only in you is my true salvation. Lord, today I remember the wounds you endured for my freedom. My sins caused you pain and suffering and you did this willingly for me to be free. So as I touch your wounds I ask that you would heal me of mine. Lord, show me where the scar tissue of my heart needs to soften. Please give me a tender, responsive heart. Forgive me that I've tried to hide my wounds away from you to protect myself. I see that hasn't helped. Lord, please heal me today. Amen.

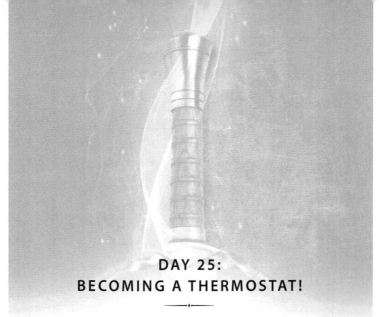

DAY 25:
BECOMING A THERMOSTAT!

———•———

"The words of the godly encourage many, but fools are destroyed
by their lack of common sense."
(Proverbs 10:21)

One Sunday in Watford, a visiting preacher and friend of ours came to minister in the church. He brought a great message and used some illustrations that really caught my imagination and have stuck with me since. He said that as children of God we should be more like thermostats than thermometers. A thermometer simply reports the temperature, but a thermostat sets it.

In spiritual terms then, a thermometer will give us information on the culture and the condition of the environment, whereas a thermostat will be able to adjust the environmental conditions. The challenge our friend brought was for us not to be head-shakers and "tutters" who give a commentary on the state of our lives and the culture we live in but, as the children of God, to carry His presence wherever we go and allow Him, through us, to change the culture. Let's adjust the temperature!

If they'd had thermostats in Jesus' day, then He may well have used a similar illustration. Instead He used common images of the day and spoke about salt and light.

Salt was not just used to season food and bring out the flavour, it was the best preservative available. Since there were no refrigerators, food was preserved by being packed in salt. Jesus said,

"You are the salt of the earth. But what good is salt if it has lost its flavour? Can you make it salty again? It will be thrown out and trampled underfoot as worthless. You are the light of the world— like a city on a hilltop that cannot be hidden. No one lights a lamp and then puts it under a basket. Instead, a lamp is placed on a stand, where it gives light to everyone in the house. In the same way, let your good deeds shine out for all to see, so that everyone will praise your heavenly Father." (Matthew 5:13-16)

Salt is apparently a very stable ingredient which, if stored dry, will not easily lose its saltiness. However, if salt is allowed to get wet then its molecular structure will alter in such a way that it loses its saltiness.

We are not meant to "dissolve" into the world. Rather we are meant to be "seasoning" – an addition to the world that brings out its best parts. We are meant to enhance the flavour of the world and not become diluted by it.

In the same way Jesus said we are meant to be like a light – a force that illuminates truth in the world and helps others to see it. We are intended to be a light that shows others which way to go.

The enemy would like us to be those who helplessly report on the circumstances of the world, powerless to affect it, but Jesus says that we can influence it in a far greater way.

When Jesus was preparing to send out His twelve disciples to go from village to village, preaching the word, healing the sick, raising the dead and casting out demons, He clearly had community transformation in His heart. He sent them out to be the salt and light that the people needed; vessels of transformation. Whatever situation they found themselves in was an opportunity to be agents of change and demonstrate the power of God.

It is allowing the Father to speak through us wherever we find ourselves that will enable us to be culture thermostats! Our God is the God of transformation. As John wrote, *"God did not send his son into the world to judge the world, but to save the world through him."* (John 3:17)

Jesus spoke of the influence that His disciples would have in their world:

"You will stand trial before governors and kings because you are my followers. But this will be your opportunity to tell the rulers and other unbelievers about me. When you are arrested, don't worry about how to respond or what to say. God will give you the right words at the right time. For it is not you who will be speaking—it will be the Spirit of your Father speaking through you." (Matthew 10:18-20)

So today, let us shake off the enemy's lies that we are helpless or have nothing to say. Let us shake off the lie that tells us we can only observe humanity's brokenness and offer a report. Instead, let us be the salt, the light, the thermostat to change our community for His glory.

It is written:

"God has given each of you a gift from his great variety of spiritual gifts. Use them well to serve one another. Do you have the gift of speaking? Then speak as though God himself were speaking through you. Do you have the gift of helping others? Do it with all the strength and energy that God supplies. Then everything you do will bring glory to God through Jesus Christ. All glory and power to him forever and ever!" (1 Peter 4:10-11)

———•———

Let's pray...

Lord, forgive me for the times when I've simply reported about the world rather than being a witness for you, since you came to save the world. Lord, today will you show me ways that I can serve you wholeheartedly, being your thermostat, to be part of your plan for the transformation of the world, through love. Lord, help me speak the truth in love about you. Help me help the world you came to love in such a way that your glory is displayed through me today. Amen.

DAY 26:
HIGHWAY OF HOLINESS

"The Lord is watching everywhere, keeping his eye on both the evil and the good."
(Proverbs 15:3)

The prophet Isaiah wrote about the hope of restoration – that life would break out, even in the wilderness, because of Jesus coming to the world.

"When he comes, he will open the eyes of the blind and unplug the ears of the deaf. The lame will leap like a deer, and those who cannot speak will sing for joy! Springs will gush forth in the wilderness, and streams will water the wasteland. The parched ground will become a pool, and springs of water will satisfy the thirsty land. Marsh grass and reeds and rushes will flourish where desert jackals once lived. And a great road will go through that once deserted land. It will be named the Highway of Holiness. Evil-minded people will never travel on it. It will be only for those who walk in God's ways; fools will never walk there." (Isaiah 35:6-8)

What a stunning passage of hope and joy.

When Jesus was tempted in the wilderness, even though the enemy wanted to lure Him away to the low place, He was committed to walking on the Highway of Holiness. Even in the wilderness, even in a place of trial, the Lord was not going to depart from His designated path.. Similarly, as we journey into victory, even in wildernesses, we can journey on the Lord's Highway of Holiness.

To understand the beauty of this passage we need to consider a few things about how and where Jesus walked for us to fully understand this invitation to victory. Jesus left the glory and wonder of heaven for our sake! So He had already lowered Himself from the highest of heights to earth's terrain. As He said Himself, *"For I have come down from heaven to do the will of God who sent me, not to do my own will. And this is the will of God, that I should not lose even one of all those he has given me, but that I should raise them up at the last day. For it is my Father's will that all who see his Son and believe in him should have eternal life. I will raise them up at the last day."* (John 6:38-40)

Though He was the Redeemer of humanity, during His time on earth Jesus walked a lowly path, stepping down to raise up those who were crushed by life, rewriting their destiny as He invited them to follow Him.

Following the path of Jesus' Highway of Holiness is a walk of humility and compassion. It has nothing to do with taking the moral high-road, where pitfalls of arrogance and judgment await. As the prophet Micah wrote: *"O people, the Lord has told you what is good, and this is what he requires of you: to do what is right, to love mercy, and to walk humbly with your God"* (Micah 6:8).

Two Christian sisters imprisoned in a Nazi concentration camp for helping to hide Jewish refugees in the war torn Netherlands in 1944 faced atrocities of unspeakable extremes. Corrie Ten Boom wrote of her story in The Hiding Place, recording that even in this terrible place, Betsie Ten Boom whispered to her sister Corrie on her death bed that, "There is no pit so deep, that God's love is not deeper still."

Jesus brought Himself down to our level so that He could rescue us. He knew that He would be broken and wounded for our sins. He had come to embrace humanity on heaven's rescue mission. There is truly no pit where He can't reach us because Jesus descended in order to lift us up. He restores us to a relationship with the Father and allows us to walk humbly on his Highway of Holiness, forgiven, restored and redeemed.

The enemy constantly tries to trap us and tells us that we are beyond the point of rescue, but that is a lie. Today there is victory for you because of the victory Jesus won on the cross, completing His rescue mission. Every situation can be transformed. Every chain can be broken. Every pit of despair can be overcome by Christ's love and power. As He stoops down to rescue us He puts our feet back on solid ground.

"I waited patiently for the Lord to help me, and he turned to me and heard my cry. He lifted me out of the pit of despair, out of the mud and the mire. He set my feet on solid ground and steadied me as I walked along. He has given me a new song to sing, a hymn of praise to our God. Many will see what he has done and be amazed. They will put their trust in the Lord. Oh, the joys of those who trust the Lord." (Psalm 40:1-4)

Today, are there situations that you thought were out of reach from the Lord? Reach out to Him and let Him lead you to solid ground.

It is written:

"Be strong, and do not fear, for your God is coming to destroy your enemies. He is coming to save you." (Isaiah 35:4)

Let's pray...

Lord, thank you that you gave up heaven to come to earth and that you lowered yourself for my sake, to rescue me. Thank you Lord that there is no circumstance, however entrapped I might feel, that is beyond your reach. I am never beyond your grasp of love. Today Lord, I choose to let you lift me and set me on solid ground. I choose to follow you on your Highway of Holiness, that my life might display your glory. Amen.

Be Victorious

Section 3: Putting God First … Really! (days 27-40)

"Again, the devil took him to a very high mountain and showed him all the kingdoms of the world and their splendour. 'All this I will give you,' he said, 'if you will bow down and worship me.' Jesus said to him, 'Away from me, Satan! For it is written: "Worship the Lord your God, and serve him only."'" (Matthew 4:8-10)

We live in a celebrity culture with a multiplicity of dazzling diversions keen to get our gaze. How do we truly put God first in our life when there are so many other priorities and people? We will be exploring the things that keep us from loving God the most, and tackling the comparison trap that keeps us from the freedom we might enjoy, as well as the double-mindedness that can hold us back.

DAY 27:
FIRST ... JUST BECAUSE

"Guard your heart above all else, for it determines the course of your life."
(Proverbs 4:23)

One of the enemy's schemes is to cause those following Christ to compromise. Jesus Himself was tempted in the wilderness to compromise on what He knew to be true, yet Jesus was without sin.

There is a wonderful story in the Old Testament of three men, friends of Daniel, who were caught up in their community's requirements to bow to the king's statue. King Nebuchadnezzar had commissioned a 90ft tall, 9ft wide, statue of himself made out of gold and demanded that everyone in his kingdom should bow in worship and adoration. But these three men were committed members of the people of God and worshipped only the Lord. They would bow to Him alone. In Philippians 3:20 Paul says, *"We are citizens of heaven, where the Lord Jesus Christ lives."* When you are a citizen of heaven you have a higher calling; you worship the Lord, forsaking the gods or idols that the world worships. This is the view these godly men held.

However, for the young men – Shadrach, Meshach and

Abednego – there would be consequences for not bowing to the king's idol. The punishment for anyone who disobeyed was to be thrown into a blazing furnace. The three men wouldn't compromise and so were arrested and brought before the enraged king.

"Then Nebuchadnezzar flew into a rage and ordered that Shadrach, Meshach, and Abednego be brought before him. When they were brought in, Nebuchadnezzar said to them, 'Is it true, Shadrach, Meshach, and Abednego, that you refuse to serve my gods or to worship the gold statue I have set up? I will give you one more chance to bow down and worship the statue I have made when you hear the sound of the musical instruments. But if you refuse, you will be thrown immediately into the blazing furnace. And then what god will be able to rescue you from my power?'" (Daniel 3:13-15)

Notice that God's power was brought into question as a result of the men's actions – as if that could determine how powerful God is.

Their response is brilliant!

"Shadrach, Meshach, and Abednego replied, 'O Nebuchadnezzar, we do not need to defend ourselves before you. If we are thrown into the blazing furnace, the God whom we serve is able to save us. He will rescue us from your power, Your Majesty. But even if he doesn't, we want to make it clear to you, Your Majesty, that we will never serve your gods or worship the gold statue you have set up.'" (Daniel 3:16-18)

They were committed to holiness. Whether God answered their prayers or not, the trial they faced was not going to determine either their obedience or the Lord's sovereignty. Our obedience should never be determined by what God does or doesn't do for us.

The Word of God is likened to a double edged sword. Using that image, I like to think that one side is named "Our God is able" and the other "But even if He doesn't". In other words, our faith is not dependent on what God does for us, but who He is to us.

The next scene in this story, however, is the men's miraculous deliverance:

"Nebuchadnezzar jumped up in amazement and exclaimed to his advisers, 'Didn't we tie up three men and throw them into the furnace?' 'Yes, Your Majesty, we certainly did,' they replied. 'Look!' Nebuchadnezzar shouted. 'I see four men, unbound, walking around in the fire unharmed! And the fourth looks like a god!' Then Nebuchadnezzar came as close as he could to the door of the flaming furnace and shouted: 'Shadrach, Meshach, and Abednego, servants of the Most High God, come out! Come here!' So Shadrach, Meshach, and Abednego stepped out of the fire. Then the high officers, officials, governors, and advisers crowded around them and saw that the fire had not touched them. Not a hair on their heads was singed, and their clothing was not scorched. They didn't even smell of smoke!" (Daniel 3:24-27)

As we walk in obedience to the Lord, He doesn't leave us to go through fiery trials alone, He walks through them with us. He wants to be right in the middle of the trials and challenges we face. When we find ourselves in the wilderness, Jesus is always close by. We cannot go through it without Him if He is the one we are following.

We might not have a 90ft golden idol to contend with, but there are plenty of other things that demand our attention and adoration. Think about what things tend to draw your gaze and occupy your thoughts. Another challenge can be unanswered prayers, which are often a source of great discouragement, but freedom can come in recognising that and choosing to trust anyway. Following God because of who He is, rather than what

He might or might not do for you, is a response that will be greeted with His favour and blessing.

The advice of the Bible is to turn all our worries into prayers and focus on God first. Then all our other needs will be looked after.

"Seek the Kingdom of God above all else, and live righteously, and he will give you everything you need." (Matthew 6:33)

Today, consider what you have planned for your day and how you can go through it putting God first in all things. Does anything need to change in order for you to put worshipping God above your own priorities and needs?

It is written:

"God blesses those who do not turn away because of me." (Matthew 11:6)

Let's pray…

Father, today I choose to put you first and to follow you in all that I do, say and think. Even if you are not doing what I had hoped you would do, or thought you might do, I will choose to follow you. Holy Spirit, fill me afresh that I might seek first the Kingdom of God. As I seek you, might you reveal more and more to me of what you see. May I see things as you see them, and think as you think. I want to become more like you. Amen.

DAY 28:
MARY'S PRAYER

———•———

"Seek his will in all you do, and he will show you which path to take."

(Proverbs 3:6)

Jesus was sent by the Father to enter our world as a human in order to become our Messiah. There was a purpose to His life. Yet, in the wilderness the enemy tempted Him to throw it all away. Jesus was tempted to worship the enemy, to give in to the pressure and succumb to idolatry. The enemy wanted to hijack Jesus' future glory and all the Lord's plans for His children's restoration. So often the enemy tries to intervene in our destiny by tripping us up before we even start.

In an encounter with the angel Gabriel a young woman's life was completely transformed. Mary, betrothed to be married to Joseph, was suddenly invited to become the recipient of the Holy Spirit in such a way that she would become the mother of Christ, the Messiah Himself. In her brief conversation with the angel, Mary moved from shock to submission with an incredible declaration of trust. Joseph received his own heavenly visitation and decided to go ahead with the marriage. The wedding plans continued, but had been incredibly upgraded in the process. Their lives went from "normal" to "extraordinary" in the moment of their submission to the Holy Spirit.

In Luke's gospel the angel of the Lord clarifies exactly how it will happen:

"The angel replied, 'The Holy Spirit will come upon you, and the power of the Most High will overshadow you. So the baby to be born will be holy, and he will be called the Son of God.'" (Luke 1:35)

To be "overshadowed" by something or someone is to become less prominent or less important than the other. Mary allowed herself to become less important; to let her will and desires become less prominent than the Lord's. As a result, she had the incredible honour of becoming the carrier of the Christ, the Saviour of humanity.

I'm sure there were loads of people around at the time who had an opinion about Mary and her future – her parents, her future in-laws, of course Joseph, and not forgetting the inquisitive neighbours. Yet this young girl, who was possibly as young as twelve years, given the culture of the day, chose to consider God's opinion more important than anyone else's.

Mary's response of submission and trust is expressed out loud as she says, *"May everything you have said about me come true"* (Luke 1:38).

In the same way, the apostle Paul let his life become overshadowed by the Lord when he realised the true identity of Jesus and submitted his life to His lordship.

"Yes, everything else is worthless when compared with the infinite value of knowing Christ Jesus my Lord. For his sake I have discarded everything else, counting it all as garbage, so that I could gain Christ and become one with him. I no longer count on my own righteousness through obeying the law; rather, I become righteous

through faith in Christ. For God's way of making us right with himself depends on faith." (Philippians 3:8-10)

Paul understood that, like Mary, he too had become a carrier of Christ in a supernatural way, since Christ now lived within him.

"So I died to the law—I stopped trying to meet all its requirements—so that I might live for God. 'My old self has been crucified with Christ. It is no longer I who live, but Christ lives in me. So I live in this earthly body by trusting in the Son of God, who loved me and gave himself for me. I do not treat the grace of God as meaningless." (Galatians 2:20-21)

When I was in my twenties I spent a long summer in El Paso, Texas, working with Youth With A Mission. It was a turning point in life as my degree was just about to enter its final year, and a significant relationship had come to an end. I was helping out in the YWAM centre preparing for some visitors when I felt the Holy Spirit begin to draw my attention. I sat in a small room, where I was meant to be collecting some linen, and became overwhelmed by an uncertain future. I began to cry. I looked at a poster on the wall which was of a long line of nappy-wearing babies. The babies were so diverse and yet all so beautiful. I remember crying out to the Lord with a burden for future generations, yearning for His will to be done in my life. I privately gave the Holy Spirit permission to overshadow me; to let what He wanted to happen in my life, actually happen. Interestingly, this launched me into a year of significant battles, where my destiny was fiercely contested, but one in which the Lord brought victory.

I'm not sure how I would have responded had an angel appeared in this linen room, or if the poster of cute babies suddenly became an angelic choir. However, today can we respond to a heavenly invitation to be overshadowed. Like Mary, our response can be, *"I am the Lord's servant. May everything you have said about me come true."* (Luke 1:38)

I want whatever the Lord has planned for my life to come to pass. I don't want any human ambitions to get in the way of the Father's will. What He says! That's what I want for my life.

Today, let's be people who, like David, recognise God's purposes in our life so that we trust Him more, knowing that He is involved in every detail of our lives. As it is written:

"Every day of my life was recorded in your book. Every moment was laid out before a single day has passed." (Psalm 139:16)

———•———

Let's pray...

Lord, help me to lean into your purposes and hear your plans for my life. May I be a person who trusts what you say about me more than what anyone else says. May I know your voice, trust your purposes and follow your lead. May everything you have said about me come true. Amen.

DAY 29:
NOWHERE TO HIDE

"Charm is deceptive, and beauty does not last; but a woman who fears the Lord will be greatly praised."
(Proverbs 30:31)

In his day Saul was apparently the most handsome man in all of Israel, standing out in any crowd due his impressive stature and good looks. Around this time Israel was pleading with the Lord to give them a new king. God's provision was Saul. During a divinely appointed adventure that included losing and finding donkeys, Saul encountered the prophet Samuel. Samuel embarks on a conversation about kingship and tells the young Saul that he and his family are God's focus for Israel's hope. Saul, however, feels his own inadequacy:

"But I'm only from the tribe of Benjamin, the smallest tribe in Israel, and my family is the least important of all the families of that tribe! Why are you talking to me about this?" (1 Samuel 9:21)

This tall man in everyone else's eyes appeared very small in his own.

Undeterred and committed to obedience, Samuel prepares to anoint Saul with oil as the new king, publically affirming his calling. Before his anointing could be recognised in public, however, God needed to meet with Saul privately and give him a new heart. The real turning point would come when Saul was transformed on the inside.

Samuel is preparing to anoint Saul in public when everyone realises Saul is missing! In a bizarre game of hide and seek the Lord snitches on Saul and reveals, *"'He is in hiding among the baggage.' So they found him and brought him out, and he stood head and shoulders above anyone else."* (1 Samuel 10:22-23)

An external anointing does not bypass the need for a transformed heart. Furthermore, heart transformation by the Lord is not a one-off occurrence but a journey that takes a lifetime. Sadly for Saul, and for Israel, Saul's heart was never fully submitted to the Lord. Though he had been chosen, he was not willing to obey the Lord, and as such the Lord rejected him as king.

Hiding from the Lord prevents healing in the Lord.

Looking beyond his impressive exterior, the Lord was always more concerned with the condition of Saul's heart. Saul never grasped this. Some time later the state of his heart deteriorated further and the Lord said to Samuel, *"Don't judge by his appearance or height, for I have rejected him. The Lord doesn't see things the way you see them. People judge by outward appearance, but the Lord looks at the heart"* (1 Samuel 16:7)

Saul unsuccessfully tried to hide his over-sized body behind some bags, in what was arguably a wonderful piece of physical comedy. Tragically, however, he also thought he could hide the condition of his soul from God too. The profundity of this knowledge was not lost on Saul's successor, David, who later wrote these words:

"O Lord, you have examined my heart and know everything

about me. You know when I sit down or stand up. You know my thoughts even when I'm far away. You see me when I travel and when I rest at home. You know everything I do. You know what I am going to say even before I say it, Lord. You go before me and follow me. You place your hand of blessing on my head. Such knowledge is too wonderful for me, too great for me to understand! I can never escape from your Spirit! I can never get away from your presence! If I go up to heaven, you are there; if I go down to the grave, you are there. If I ride the wings of the morning, if I dwell by the farthest oceans, even there your hand will guide me, and your strength will support me. I could ask the darkness to hide me and the light around me to become night— but even in darkness I cannot hide from you. To you the night shines as bright as day. Darkness and light are the same to you." (Psalm 139:1-12)

Unlike Saul, David recognised God's omniscience and omnipresence as a wonderful blessing. He submitted his heart to the Lord and committed himself to a path of obedience. David's story is part-two in the drama of two unlikely men, both called by God to servant-kingship, whose response to the Lord were diametrically opposed.

Many of us have considered the insignificance of our backgrounds or the facts of our circumstances to be factors that disqualify us from stepping into the purposes of God for our lives. Knowing our latent potential, the enemy is delighted when we waver from trusting God. He is no doubt thrilled when we choose to hide, even though doing so is futile, and we miss our destiny. Profoundly, when we try to hide from God we are more exposed and vulnerable to our enemies.

David realised something simply wonderful though. Instead of hiding *from* God, where we are vulnerable to attack, we can hide *in* God and there be protected from our enemies.

"*The one thing I ask of the Lord— the thing I seek most—is to live in the house of the Lord all the days of my life, delighting in the Lord's perfections and meditating in his Temple. For he will conceal me there when troubles come; he will hide me in his sanctuary. He will place me out of reach on a high rock. Then I will hold my head high above my enemies who surround me. At his sanctuary I will offer sacrifices with shouts of joy, singing and praising the Lord with music. Hear me as I pray, O Lord. Be merciful and answer me! My heart has heard you say, 'Come and talk with me.' And my heart responds, 'Lord, I am coming.'*" (Psalm 127:4-8)

Have you been trying to hide yourself, or anything, from God? Think about how you can hide within Him and not from Him today.

Let us respond to the Lord's invitation to come and talk to Him. Draw near to Him. Hide in Him. Realise that there is nowhere we can run from Him and instead run to Him – the safest place of all.

It is written:

"*He will conceal me when troubles come; he will hide me in his sanctuary.*" (Psalm 127:5)

———•———

Let's pray...

Father, there are so many times when I feel like I'm small and insignificant, yet you choose to call me to be with you, to be your child and to walk with you. Today I want to come and talk with you. Help me to keep being with you all day. Please hide me in you, so that the troubles around me will pass me by. Thank you that there is nowhere I can hide from you and that you can always protect me. Lord, today I praise you that you are my safe place. Amen.

DAY 30:
REFINER'S FIRE

———•———

"Fire tests the purity of silver and gold, but the Lord tests the heart."
(Proverbs 17:3)

The refining of gold is an incredible process that has remained largely unchanged over many centuries. The gold is heated to phenomenal temperatures so that it becomes completely molten. In this state, all its inherent dross and impurities rise to the surface where the refiner can remove them. The refiner doesn't have to stir or poke about in the gold, he simply skims the surface as layer upon layer of impurity is taken away.

The prophet Malachi refers to this ancient process when He speaks about God's desire to purify His people:

"But who will be able to endure it when he comes? Who will be able to stand and face him when he appears? For he will be like a blazing fire that refines metal, or like a strong soap that bleaches clothes. He will sit like a refiner of silver, burning away the dross. He will purify the Levites, refining them like gold and silver, so that they may once again offer acceptable sacrifices to the Lord. Then once more the Lord will accept the offerings brought to

him by the people of Judah and Jerusalem, as he did in the past." (Malachi 3:2-4)

Whilst we understand that we are made fully acceptable to God because of Jesus' sacrifice on our behalf, we still have to go through a process of maturing in our faith; of becoming increasingly more Christlike. And that involves being refined.

As Jesus journeyed through the sweltering wilderness, the heat was turned up on Him. What came to the surface was nothing but pure gold, as Jesus was without sin, but that is not our story. When the heat is turned up in our lives, we can be sure that the impurities will come to the surface.

Think of the times when you are feeling extra-tried, overworked and pulled in every direction. The heat is on. In those moments of testing, what comes to the surface? What words come out of your mouth? Paul taught us to, *"Let everything you say be good and helpful, so that your words will be an encouragement to those who hear them"* (Ephesians 4:29).

Our words reveal what is in our heart. A sure test of the quality of my heart as a disciple is the way in which I speak. It is so easy for the ugly stuff to surface in all of us. But the beauty of this is that the Great Refiner can skim away the scum and dross and cleanse our hearts.

Generally we are pretty good at presenting our "refined" face in public. In my experience, the ugly stuff tends to surface first at home. Not so long ago, for really no good reason, I was feeling irrationally angry. It was triggered by a simple conversation about my car. To be honest, I can't even remember the details – it was that trivial. However, I was spouting angry words in the direction of my husband, with my children as the "audience", overhearing my outburst from another room and probably becoming increasingly concerned about what I was doing to their tea, since I was trying to cook at the time!

After a while of ranting, I told Tim that I wasn't going to speak any more. You would have thought he'd have been thrilled that I had decided to press mute on my mouth, but for a little while longer he pushed me for a rational response. I remembered Paul's advice however, and because I couldn't say anything good, helpful or encouraging at that point, I decided to keep quiet and pray silently. Rather than continue to let the ugliness spill out, when I let Him, the Lord was able to gently remove my anger. An apology could then follow and both the situation, and my mood, were returned to a place of peace.

In the book of Lamentations the writer, most likely Jeremiah, is writing of the tragedy of Jerusalem's destruction, but he captures the essence of what it is like to come under the refiner's fire. He speaks of our necessary repentance, intercession and surrender:

"Cry aloud before the Lord, O walls of beautiful Jerusalem! Let your tears flow like a river day and night. Give yourselves no rest; give your eyes no relief. Rise during the night and cry out. Pour out your hearts like water to the Lord. Lift up your hands to him in prayer." (Lamentations 2:18-19)

Allowing our hearts to be changed from a place of hardness to our own sin to repentance, or from a place of indifference to the plight of those in need to compassion, means that God is able to refine us further still.

There are so many different trials that people go through in different seasons. I think about the trials our brothers and sisters in Christ go through in other nations, such as in Africa, suffering poverty, famine, a lack of health care, facing persecution for their faith. Closer to home the trials are different, but nonetheless challenging, with issues of health, employment, poverty, relationships, equality, disability, bereavements and family needs to name but a few. Can we surrender ourselves and trust God to shape us through such trials? Can we give ourselves to intercession for others, trusting the Lord to refine us in the heat of the trial, so that He will be glorified in and through us?

Today, don't be condemned when ugly stuff rises to the surface. The voice of condemnation is not the voice of our loving Father, it is the enemy. Allow the ugly stuff to rise to the surface as the heat of pressure increases and allow the Father to refine you as you give Him the rubbish. He's paid a high price for it.

As it is written:

"So be truly glad. There is wonderful joy ahead, even though you must endure many trials for a little while. These trials will show that your faith is genuine. It is being tested as fire tests and purifies gold—though your faith is far more precious than mere gold. So when your faith remains strong through many trials, it will bring you much praise and glory and honour on the day when Jesus Christ is revealed to the whole world." (1 Peter 1:6-7)

Let's pray…

Lord, I come to you today in the trials I am facing and pour myself out before you. Lord, please keep my heart soft that it might be like liquid gold before you. Take away any rubbish that is within me and refine me for your glory. I trust you to be with me in this trial; I trust that I will come through this refined and victorious. Amen.

DAY 31:
EYES ON THE PRIZE

"Look straight ahead, and fix your eyes on what lies before you."
(Proverbs 4:25)

In the wilderness Jesus was tempted to take His eyes off the Father and worship the enemy instead. However, Jesus' eyes were on the eternal prize.

Paul wrote about this to the church in Corinth. He imagined himself like an athlete: *"I discipline my body like an athlete, training it to do what it should. Otherwise, I fear that after preaching to others I myself might be disqualified"* (1 Corinthians 9:27).

Paul wanted to be disciplined and trained in such a way that a race could be won. Imagine for a moment you are an Olympic athlete. Choose your sport, imagine your training, focus on what you want to achieve. As an athlete, it's important to have a goal in mind if you want to run your race to win, shoot to score, or jump to clear the hurdle. Top athletes need to have incredible focus to keep the desired goal in view. Losing sight of the goal will inevitably cause a drift with often disastrous outcomes.

What we focus on can not only help us win our race, but determines how we run it. We can't afford to be distracted and have our attention pulled away to other things. Paul spoke to the Galatians about our tendency to do this: *"You were running the race so well. Who has held you back from following the truth? It certainly isn't God, for he is the one who called you to freedom"* (Galatians 5:7-8).

One challenge here is to recognise that often it's *who* not *what* is holding us back. Circumstances may distract us, but more often than not it's people. Remember the time when Jesus was fixing His eyes on His purpose and Peter got in the way.

"From then on Jesus began to tell his disciples plainly that it was necessary for him to go to Jerusalem, and that he would suffer many terrible things at the hands of the elders, the leading priests, and the teachers of religious law. He would be killed, but on the third day he would be raised from the dead. But Peter took him aside and began to reprimand him for saying such things. 'Heaven forbid, Lord,' he said. 'This will never happen to you!' Jesus turned to Peter and said, 'Get away from me, Satan! You are a dangerous trap to me. You are seeing things merely from a human point of view, not from God's.'" (Matthew 16:21-23)

I'm confident that Peter was speaking out of love and with good intentions. We all want to cling to those we love and keep them close to us for as long as possible. But though he had good intentions, Peter had missed God's intentions. Just as Eve was subtly deceived by the serpent in the Garden, so Peter was temporarily misguided. Jesus saw through this, of course, and didn't rebuke Peter but rather rebuked the devil!

Staying focussed on the purposes of the Lord will enable us to run the race and not get distracted. A friend of mine recently said, "Don't engage in every battle. If a battle is not between you and your destiny, it's simply a distraction."

Determining not to let anyone cut in on you as you run your

race, as Paul put it, is not the same as being uninterruptible. There is always an aspect of our journey with the Lord that is an adventure and somewhat unpredictable as the Holy Spirit leads us. Jesus told the story of a Samaritan man on a journey who allowed himself to be interrupted to help the needs of a Jewish man who had been mugged and left for dead. Other religious leaders had ignored the victim and travelled on their way, uninterrupted. The Samaritan, however, did what was good. He stopped. He allowed his journey to be interrupted. He helped. But it was all within the purposes of the Lord.

Victory, then, comes when we allow God alone to interrupt our plans with His. But we must never allow the enemy to disrupt our plans for his! Have you been disrupted and distracted from keeping your eyes fixed on the Lord's goals for your life?

If someone has said something to you that has "disrupted" or discouraged you, I encourage you to release forgiveness to them now. Forgiving them is not the same as saying what they did was OK, and it may still hurt for a while. Rather, forgiveness is about you getting back up and starting to run again.

Now determine to fix your eyes ahead on Christ. He has taken hold of you for a purpose. It is time to fix your eyes on Jesus.

"Since we are surrounded by such a huge crowd of witnesses to the life of faith, let us strip off every weight that slows us down, especially the sin that so easily trips us up. And let us run with endurance the race God has set before us. We do this by keeping our eyes on Jesus, the champion who imitates and perfects our faith." (Hebrews 12:1-2)

There is a beautiful victory that comes when we run our own race and don't try to run someone else's. There is freedom when we release ourselves from comparison and shake off the enemy's schemes to lead us into temptation. Father God has a plan for each of us. Keeping our eyes fixed on Jesus enables us to run according to that plan.

It is written:

"Don't be afraid, for I am with you. Don't be discouraged, for I am your God. I will strengthen you and help you. I will hold you up with my victorious right hand." (Isaiah 41:10)

———•———

Let's pray...

Father, I thank you that you have a plan for my life and you want me to run a good race with you and for you. Please help me today to focus on what is ahead. Today I choose to keep my eyes on you and shake off any distractions or burdens which will weigh me down. Today I run for, and with, you Jesus. Amen.

DAY 32:
DON'T LOOK BACK

"Don't turn your back on wisdom, for she will protect you. Love her, and she will guard you."
(Proverbs 4:6)

On a recent family holiday we were enjoying a family walk down a country lane. Leading the way, one of our children turned round to talk to us while continuing to walk, and so ended up walking backwards. This might have been fine had we not been on a narrow lane and had there not been a car heading our way. Sudden shouts from those of us walking who were looking in the right direction averted a potentially terrible accident.

Travelling forwards while constantly looking back is a sure way of falling over and getting hurt. Fixing our eyes on the goal ahead means that we can't constantly look over our shoulder at where we've come from.

In Genesis we read the tragic story of a rescue that went sadly wrong. Lot and his wife were being rescued from sure destruction in Sodom and Gomorrah. They were clearly instructed by the angel of the Lord not to look back as they left the city. Lot's wife did not obey. Perhaps the intrigue, or remorse, or the pull of bereavement caused her to look upon the destruction. Maybe the screams and sounds of demolition drew her attention. Perhaps it was the pull of the past, the thought of leaving the familiar behind, not really knowing what the future held. Whatever compelled her to look back, her disobedience cost her everything as she was turned into a pillar of salt. This was not what the Lord had in mind when He encouraged us to keep salty!

I've pastored people over the years who have enjoyed such amazing times in the past that they live in the memory of their former glory. One couple I ministered to had had such incredible spiritual experiences at university that nothing since had ever felt the same. Decades later they were still missing the "good old days". Others may have had the opposite experience, but the pain of their past still keep them looking back rather than focusing on the future. In addition, the more years we've lived, the more we can think that our best days are behind us. Of course, this is not really the case. Eternity is ahead, so with our eyes on heaven and our eternal future we can confidently say that truly the best is yet to come.

God said, through the prophet Isaiah,

"I am the Lord, your Holy One, Israel's Creator and King. I am the Lord, who opened a way through the waters, making a dry path through the sea. I called forth the mighty army of Egypt with all its chariots and horses. I drew them beneath the waves, and they drowned, their lives snuffed out like a smouldering candlewick. But forget all that— it is nothing compared to what I am going to do. For I am about to do something new. See, I have already begun! Do you not see it? I will make a pathway through the wilderness. I will create rivers in the dry wasteland. The wild animals in the fields will thank me, the jackals and owls, too, for giving them water in the desert. Yes, I will make rivers in the dry wasteland so my chosen

people can be refreshed." (Isaiah 43:15-20)

Jesus also identified the challenge of pressing on in pursuit of following God when He talked to someone who had declared their intention to always follow Him. Jesus pointed out that there would be a cost to keep following and not turning back. He said, *"anyone who puts a hand to the plough and then looks back is not fit for the Kingdom of God"* (Luke 9:62).

To take hold of the future it is necessary to let go of any part of our past that holds us back.

John tells a story in his gospel of a lady caught in adultery, who is dragged before Jesus. The religious leaders are demanding that the consequences of the law are invoked. The people were baying for a stoning and Jesus was being tested. *"They were trying to trap him into saying something they could use against him, but Jesus stooped down and wrote in the dust with his finger"* (John 8:6-7)

What Jesus wrote is widely speculated upon but remains emphatically uncertain. But in that moment He drew the gaze off the woman as He informed the crowd that only the person who had never sinned could throw the first stone. As each of her accusers skulked away and disappeared into the shadows, Jesus turned to the woman and said, *"'Where are your accusers? Didn't even one of them condemn you?' 'No, Lord,' she said. And Jesus said, 'Neither do I. Go and sin no more'"* (John 8:10-11)

Jesus draws a line in the sand for us to cross over; to know that He is the one who silences the voice of the accuser. He longs to lavish His grace and love upon us, not condemning us but forgiving us and inviting us into our destiny.

Today, consider all that Jesus has done in your life and, with a grateful heart, acknowledge what has brought you to this point. If the enemy seeks to accuse you of your past sins, let Jesus silence him for you. Look to Jesus. Look ahead with thanks. Jesus is calling you to follow Him, so that you will move forward and receive the prize that lies ahead.

As Jesus said, it is written:

"My sheep listen to my voice; and I know them, and they follow me." (John 10:27)

Let's pray…

Thank you, Lord, for all the great things in my past. I even thank you for the challenges that have helped shape who I am today. Thank you for all the times you have made a way when there has been no way. Lord, today I choose to look forward and look towards the heavenly prize which you have planned for me. I choose to be grateful for the past, but expectant for the future. Thank you that I can know your voice. Help me to hear your voice today clearer than any other. Thank you that you know me. I choose to follow you today. Amen.

DAY 33:
THE HIGHER POWER

"The wise conquer the city of the strong and level the fortress in which they trust."
(Proverbs 21:22)

As Jesus journeyed through the wilderness, so the enemy was roaming about too, seeking an opportunity to test and tempt the Lord. The enemy clearly has a certain amount of freedom to move around and act as if he is in charge, seeking to maximise his limited power and authority. Whilst Jesus was *led* into the wilderness by the Spirit, He was then *taken* to the high mountain by the devil. Even fully submitted to the Father, the Lord Jesus was able to be taken by the devil. This was clearly not against Jesus' will, however, as if a hostage to the enemy, but rather it was permitted.

Jesus knew the limitations of the enemy and was well aware of His Father's higher power. Three years later Jesus was facing false accusations before Pilate, at the time of His trial. Pilate appears exasperated by the position he finds himself in, being forced to condemn a man he discerns has done no wrong, whilst at the same time not wanting to incite further trouble from the baying mob.

The crowd is shouting for Jesus' blood and Pilate is concerned that Jesus is not helping him to release Him. Challenging Him, Pilate says, *"Don't you realise that I have the power to release you or crucify you?"* (John 19:10). He tries to provoke Jesus into a more helpful response. However, Jesus recognises that whilst things look as though they are spiralling out of control on a human level, the sovereign power of God is at work. A greater power, a higher authority and a bigger plan are all being out-worked. John records Jesus' words: *"You would have no power over me at all unless it were given to you from above"* (John 19:11).

Paul referred to Satan as the *"god of this world"* (2 Corinthians 4:4) , but we understand the bigger picture from the psalmist's writings:

"For the Lord is a great God, a great King above all gods. He holds in his hands the depths of the earth and the mightiest mountains. The sea belongs to him, for he made it. His hands formed the dry land, too." (Psalm 95:3-5)

As a consequence of original sin in the Garden of Eden, the Lord cursed the enemy to crawl on his belly like a serpent, and spoke of the hostility that would exist between him and mankind forever more. Foretelling the coming of Christ, the Lord said that, *"He will strike your head, and you will strike his heel"* (Genesis 3:15). The devil could afflict Christ's humanity whilst on earth, but the victory ultimately belongs to Jesus who crushes the head of the enemy and brings an end to his reign of terror.

Having something snapping at your heels while you try to walk is a sure way of tripping up and falling over. When my kids were little, a favourite game that worked particularly well on wooden or tiled floors, was for them to lie on their tummies holding our ankles. We would then attempt to walk as they hung on tight and slid around. Normally this was great fun, but as they got bigger, it was harder to drag them around and occasionally, an unexpected move on their part threatened to trip up their parents!

The image of the enemy grabbing at the heels of mankind, trying to wound us and cause us to stumble is a striking one. Our enemy is not playing childish games with us; he is set on our destruction. He knows it is very difficult for us to walk with him grabbing at our feet. Because of Jesus, however, we need not be tripped up or held back by the enemy's tactics. Jesus explained the true order of things to His disciples:

"I saw Satan fall from heaven like lightning! Look, I have given you authority over all the power of the enemy, and you can walk among snakes and scorpions and crush them. Nothing will injure you. But don't rejoice because evil spirits obey you; rejoice because your names are registered in heaven." (Luke 10:18-20)

Jesus has won the victory for us, so that we can walk unhindered. The enemy can be kept underfoot. When he tempted Jesus the enemy was only able to operate within a limited capacity of authority. The same is still true today. Jesus wanted His disciples then, and us now, to know that we have delegated authority from Him that gives us authority over the works of the evil one. When Jesus gathered His disciples together He gave them "authority to cast out evil spirits and to heal every kind of disease and illness" (Matthew 10:1).

In the wilderness Jesus didn't bow in worship to the enemy, knowing full well that in the future it would be he who was forced to bend the knee. Jesus didn't need to give up His authority for a quick fix of earthly glory – rather He would wait until He, in His heavenly glory, would see the enemy defeated.

Today consider the glorious power of Jesus that enables us to walk amongst the "snakes" and still know His victory. For it is written:

"*Therefore, God elevated him to the place of highest honour and gave him the name above all other names, that at the name of Jesus every knee should bow, in heaven and on earth and under the earth, and every tongue declare that Jesus Christ is Lord, to the glory of God the Father.*" (Philippians 2:9-11)

———•———

Let's pray...

Lord Jesus, I thank you that it is all about you. Jesus, because of what you have done on the cross you have enabled us to walk amongst our enemy and know that we can be victorious. Your name is the most powerful of all names and because of you we can be completely free from the enemy's grasp. In your name we are victorious. Amen.

DAY 34:
JESUS IS NOT A GENIE!

———•———

"Many seek the ruler's favour, but justice comes from the Lord."
(Proverbs 29:26)

Jesus was tempted to worship the enemy for His own (supposed) gain. Today the enemy still tempts us to pursue our own agendas, seeking to draw our worship away from God. The challenge comes when we think that we know better than God what we need. I'm sure many of us would do things differently to Him, given the chance. I know that if I were God (a scary thought indeed, but it's OK, I'm not!), I would have definitely done quite a few things differently in my life and the lives of those around me.

Remember the Disney film *Aladdin*? It's the story of a young, "rough diamond" who stumbles into his own love story with a princess. Along the way a magic lamp comes into his possession. The genie of the lamp can grant him three wishes – anything he desires! We may never have wished for outrageous things like Aladdin, but I think that sometimes we treat God like He's a genie. It's not a comfortable thought, but hear me out. Sometimes we approach God because we just want Him to grant our wishes, meet our needs, to do things the way we want Him to do things.

Then we feel frustrated when He doesn't do the things we want, or in the way we wanted them done.

Have you ever done this? I have, for sure! God has not answered my prayers in the way I would have liked on more than one occasion!

Often God does not act as we expect Him to. Consider Jesus' cousin, John the Baptist. John spent many years living in extreme conditions as a living signpost to the imminent arrival of Jesus, the Messiah. His whole life's mission was to prepare the way for Jesus. No sooner had the public ministry of Jesus gotten started than John was arrested, never to set foot outside of captivity again. From prison, John sent two of his disciples to question Jesus, to check whether He really was "the one" John had been prophesying about. Why? Maybe it was because the Jesus who came didn't match John's preconceived ideas. Many expected the Messiah to be a political and military leader. Jesus wasn't that. Jesus wasn't busy making everything comfortable for the people of God. He hadn't used His power to spring John out of jail. What was going on?

Jesus was, however, happy to answer John's questions:

"Then he told John's disciples, 'Go back to John and tell him what you have seen and heard—the blind see, the lame walk, the lepers are cured, the deaf hear, the dead are raised to life, and the Good News is being preached to the poor. And tell him, "God blesses those who do not turn away because of me."'" (Luke 7:22-23)

Jesus knew that some people would be tempted to give up on Him because He wasn't doing what they wanted Him to do in the way that they wanted Him to do it. In other words, Jesus was not being their genie to grant wishes.

The enemy would like us to fall into the trap of questioning God because our prayers don't seem to get answered. The real trap, however, is the one that keeps us thinking that God is somehow our personal genie, whose role in life is to grant our wishes. Freedom comes when we submit to God's love, put Him first, and then bring to Him all our needs with faith and expectation, because He is a good Father. Remember that even Jesus didn't get a prayer answered in the way He would have preferred:

"Father, if you are willing, please take this cup of suffering away from me. Yet I want your will to be done, not mine." (Luke 7:42)

Victory comes to us when we overcome the enemy's temptation to put ourselves ahead of God. God's will must be done above ours. We must trust that He knows what He is doing; He knows what is best for us.

If you are going through a difficult season presently, know that in time it will pass. As a parent there have been numerous occasions when my children, especially when little, have struggled to understand why they had to go through a difficult situation. Why didn't God just wave His hand and take it away? I explained to them that they wouldn't be stuck in this season forever. My experience has always been that *this too shall pass*. It's something Paul understood and wrote to the believers in Corinth about, encouraging them to have a longer-term perspective:

"For our present troubles are small and won't last very long. Yet they produce for us a glory that vastly outweighs them and will last forever! So we don't look at the troubles we can see now; rather, we fix our gaze on things that cannot be seen. For the things we see now will soon be gone, but the things we cannot see will last forever." (2 Corinthians 4:17-18)

We could debate what is meant by the word "soon". As John wrote in Revelation,

"Look, I am coming soon, bringing my reward with me to repay all people according to their deeds. I am the Alpha and the Omega,

the First and the Last, the Beginning and the End." (Revelation 22:12-13)

Though we can't define "soon", and it may not be as soon as we'd like it to be, we take comfort from the fact that the Lord is the one who knows "the beginning and the end". He wants us to sharpen our swords, stand on His truth, lift our eyes heavenward and not stumble when He doesn't do things quite the way we expected. Instead, we will worship Him, trust Him completely, and ask for His will to be done, not ours.

Today, let's put aside the thought that God should be granting our wishes, or that He somehow exists in order to make our lives better. These thoughts are a trap of the enemy. Instead we choose to trust God.

It written:

"'My thoughts are nothing like your thoughts,' says the Lord. 'And my ways are far beyond anything you could imagine. For just as the heavens are higher than the earth, so my ways are higher than your ways and my thoughts higher than your thoughts.'" (Isaiah 55:8-9)

———•———

Let's pray...

Lord, help me to trust you and let go of any disappointment for unanswered prayers. Help me to submit to your will and worship you first in my life. Help me to seek your thoughts and your ways. Thank you that you know the beginning from the end, so I choose to trust you. Amen.

DAY 35:
POTTY FOR THE POTTER

"But all who listen to me will live in peace, untroubled by fear of harm."
(Proverbs 1:33)

The creation narrative describes the beautiful scenes of creation as the formless, empty earth begins to burst with life. Light and dark, water, land and sky all receive their own unique fragrances, sights and sounds. Teeming with abundance the world becomes the home of animals, handcrafted from the divine imagination of God. Then the Lord begins to form humankind. *"The Lord God formed the man from the dust of the ground. He breathed the breath of life into the man's nostrils, and the man became a living person"* (Genesis 2:7). Of all the good things that the Lord created, when He looked on humankind he knew that it was very good.

What an incredible image! God breathed into the mud-man, turning what would have been a clay statue into a living human, containing the very breath of God. This is our inheritance and our identity: created by God; brought to life with His breath.

Being made in the image of our creative God means that we are all, in some way, created creative! I'm not one of those mega-creative types who can produce amazing things with my hands, but I know plenty of people who can. A former neighbour of our family makes the most outstanding doll's house miniatures – stunning, handmade, intricate and quite frankly brilliant teeny-tiny little creations: banquets of model food, intricate household items, the list is endless. It's not surprising, my friend is, after all, made in the image of the creative God who loves making things out of mud!

We are intricately and lovingly handcrafted by the Lord. Isaiah paints this beautiful picture: *"And yet, O Lord, you are our Father. We are the clay, and you are the potter. We all are formed by your hand"* (Isaiah 64:8).

We are not just clay pots though. We were created to carry something profound and each of us, whether we know it or not, has the capacity to receive the breath of God – His presence within us. Paul wrote,

"For God, who said, 'Let there be light in the darkness,' has made this light shine in our hearts so we could know the glory of God that is seen in the face of Jesus Christ. We now have this light shining in our hearts, but we ourselves are like fragile clay jars containing this great treasure. This makes it clear that our great power is from God, not from ourselves." (2 Corinthians 4:6-7)

In our Western culture we suffer from a culture that is obsessed with celebrity. In all walks of life people put other people on pedestals and following their virtual life via social media, displaying alarming adoration. Even in the sphere of Christian ministry, people are put on pedestals. As a result, many children grow up simply wanting "to be famous". They aspire to a life that someone else doesn't really live, with the myth perpetuated by tweets, status updates and photos.

Yet, we are all just jars of clay! The most profound part of us is hidden. It is what is happening on the inside that is vital – whether or not we have received the breath of God and have the light of Christ living within us. Our glory is not to be found in our human strength or any of our achievements – our glory comes from us being filled with His glory!

The prophet Jeremiah delivered a strong word from the Lord to His people, urging them to be obedient. God said to Jeremiah, *"'Go down to the potter's shop, and I will speak to you there.' So I did as he told me and found the potter working at his wheel. But the jar he was making did not turn out as he had hoped, so he crushed it into a lump of clay again and started over. Then the Lord gave me this message: 'O Israel, can I not do to you as this potter has done to his clay? As the clay is in the potter's hand, so are you in my hand.'"* (Jeremiah 8:1-6)

Jeremiah's words are a sobering reminder that we are but clay in the Potter's hands. He wants to shape us into something amazing that will bring glory to His name. Remember that Jesus taught the enemy's purpose is to *"steal and kill and destroy"*. Yet Christ's purpose is for us to receive *"a rich and satisfying life"* from Him. The Lord longs to fill our clay jars with treasures from heaven, so that His light replaces our darkness, His power replaces our weakness. He desires that His glory will overshadow our frailty, that through us the world might see Him. Jesus urged His disciples (and continues to pray the same for you and me) to, *"let your good deeds shine out for all to see, so that everyone will praise your heavenly Father"* (Matthew 5:16)

Today, the Lord looks on His creation, sees His people, and knows that they have the potential of yet again being "very good". He longs to breathe His life into us and to allow His light to shine through us. He longs for our frail selves to be filled with His glory that the world would see Him in us. Today will you let Him fill you afresh with His Holy Spirit, so that you will display His glory as you go about your day?

It is written:

"I am certain that God, who began the good work within you, will continue his work until it is finally finished on the day when Christ Jesus returns." (Philippians 1:6)

———•———

Let's pray...

Father, I thank you for your breath, and for your light that you have put in me. I thank you that you long to display your glory through my life. I thank you that no one deserves my worship more than you because all of us are just clay jars. Lord, as the Potter, will you mould me as you want me, so that my life might be everything you have created and intended it to be. Amen.

DAY 36:
CALL HIM DADDY

"My father taught me, 'Take my words to heart. Follow my commands, and you will live.'"
(Proverbs 4:4)

When I was in my teens there was a fashion, in certain circles, for children to call their parents by their first names. I think it was meant as a demonstration of equality – the parents affirming that their children were becoming adults. I recall one conversation with my dad when he asked my sister and I if we would like to call him Derek. This sounded weird to us. Not because of the name – that's his name, we'd heard it lots of times before! But because we had only ever called him Dad or Daddy. There were only two people on the planet who could rightfully call him Dad, and neither my sister nor I had any intention of giving up this right.

In Christ, we are no longer fearful slaves to sin, but children of God, who get to call our heavenly Father "Abba" (the Aramaic word for Daddy). We read that,

"Even before he made the world, God loved us and chose us in Christ to be holy and without fault in his eyes. God decided in advance to adopt us into his own family by bringing us to himself

through Jesus Christ. This is what he wanted to do, and it gave him great pleasure. So we praise God for the glorious grace he has poured out on us who belong to his dear Son. He is so rich in kindness and grace that he purchased our freedom with the blood of his Son and forgave our sins. He has showered his kindness on us, along with all wisdom and understanding." (Ephesians 1:4-8)

"I will be your Father, and you will be my sons and daughters, says the Lord Almighty." (2 Corinthians 6:18)

At Jesus' baptism He was publically affirmed by His Father as God's beloved Son. It was following on from this that Jesus was led by the Spirit into the wilderness. Paul teaches that being led by the Spirit of God is another confirmation of our status as children of God, and of the glorious inheritance we will receive.

The enemy tempted Jesus to give up His son-ship in the wilderness, but Jesus refused to give in to temptation. The enemy will tempt us to do the same, but like Jesus, we can walk secure in our identity, confident of who God says we are in Him.

"For all who are led by the Spirit of God are children of God. So you have not received a spirit that makes you fearful slaves. Instead, you received God's Spirit when he adopted you as his own children. Now we call him, 'Abba, Father.' For his Spirit joins with our spirit to affirm that we are God's children. And since we are his children, we are his heirs. In fact, together with Christ we are heirs of God's glory. But if we are to share his glory, we must also share his suffering." (Romans 8:14-16)

The King of all Kings has, through Christ, drawn us near to His throne. He has reached out, taken us into His arms, and says to us, "You can call me Daddy!"

I appreciate that readers will have a wide spectrum of experience when it comes to earthly fatherhood. For sure, none of our fathers are perfect, but Jesus says we can rely absolutely on

God. *"Your Father in heaven is perfect"* (Matthew 5:48).

Paul continued teaching the Romans saying that, *"Concerning the Gentiles, God says in the prophecy of Hosea, 'Those who were not my people, I will now call my people. And I will love those whom I did not love before.' And, 'Then, at the place where they were told, "You are not my people," there they will be called 'children of the living God.'"* (Romans 9:25-26)

From the Old to the New Testament the Lord has been on a mission of adoption. His heart is to reconnect with His children as their Daddy, not their master; not as a stranger, but as family.

Just as son-ship was at the heart of Jesus' temptation in the wilderness, the same is true for us today. Our relationship as sons and daughters of the living God will be contested, undermined, brought into question, ridiculed and misunderstood. The enemy's tactic is to sow seeds of doubt regarding who we are in Christ.

Today, consider your relationship with your earthly dad and give thanks to God for the life you have. Draw near to your heavenly Father and remember how many different blessings He has shown you. *"See how very much our Father loves us, for he calls us his children, and that is what we are!"* (1 John 3:1)

It is written:

"And because we are his children, God has sent the Spirit of his Son into our hearts, prompting us to call out, 'Abba, Father.' Now you are no longer a slave but God's own child. And since you are his child, God has made you his heir." (Galatians 4:6-7)

———•———

Let's pray...

Father, may I grow in knowing you as my Daddy. Today may I walk even more closely with you, so that I can see what you are doing and hear what you are saying. Help me to live as your child and not as a slave to fear. Help me come to you like a child and walk with you today in every way. Amen.

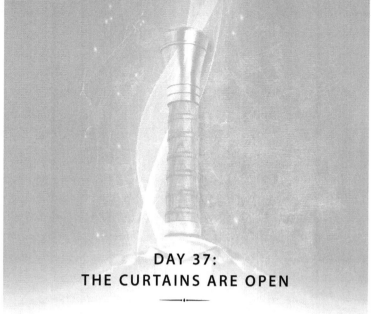

DAY 37:
THE CURTAINS ARE OPEN

"The way of the righteous is like the first gleam of dawn, which shines ever brighter until the full light of day."
(Proverbs 4:18)

Today, as I sit and write, the sun is pouring through the window, bouncing light around my room. The sky is blue and the weather is inviting. Such a difference from last night when the rain was heavy against the window and I was glad to be in the warmth of our home, firmly closing the curtains to blot out the storm. Today, I wouldn't dream of shutting my curtains and blocking out the sunshine.

In the gospel accounts of Jesus' crucifixion we read,

"Then Jesus uttered another loud cry and breathed his last. And the curtain in the sanctuary of the Temple was torn in two, from top to bottom. When the Roman officer who stood facing him saw how he had died, he exclaimed, 'This man truly was the Son of God!'"
(Mark 15:37-38)

In the original temple in Israel's past there was a curtain that separated the Holy of Holies from the outer areas. To help us understand the significance of this the writer to Hebrews exquisitely explains…

"That first covenant between God and Israel had regulations for worship and a place of worship here on earth. There were two rooms in that Tabernacle. In the first room were a lampstand, a table, and sacred loaves of bread on the table. This room was called the Holy Place. Then there was a curtain, and behind the curtain was the second room called the Most Holy Place … But we cannot explain these things in detail now. When these things were all in place, the priests regularly entered the first room as they performed their religious duties. But only the high priest ever entered the Most Holy Place, and only once a year. And he always offered blood for his own sins and for the sins the people had committed in ignorance …. For the gifts and sacrifices that the priests offer are not able to cleanse the consciences of the people who bring them. For that old system deals only with food and drink and various cleansing ceremonies— physical regulations that were in effect only until a better system could be established. So Christ has now become the High Priest over all the good things that have come. He has entered that greater, more perfect Tabernacle in heaven, which was not made by human hands and is not part of this created world. With his own blood—not the blood of goats and calves—he entered the Most Holy Place once for all time and secured our redemption forever." (Hebrews 9:1-12)

Once and for all time the curtain was torn because Christ has gone through to make it possible for us all to enter into the presence of the Father in an active and living relationship. This is irreversible, irrefutable, and for all eternity.

In my home, day follows night, light follows darkness. As a result I am always opening and closing my curtains. But in the spiritual realm, because of what Jesus accomplished on the cross, the curtain has been permanently removed. We can now rejoice in the fact that, *"the light shines in the darkness, and the darkness can never extinguish it"* (John 1:5).

In Christ, our relationship has been permanently established. It is not a temporary measure. We are not God's foster children, secure for a fleeting time before, once again, our future becomes uncertain. We are permanently adopted as God's children for all time.

Jesus sacrificed His life for us in order to secure that relationship. He said of Himself,

"I am the good shepherd; I know my own sheep, and they know me, just as my Father knows me and I know the Father. So I sacrifice my life for the sheep. I have other sheep, too, that are not in this sheepfold. I must bring them also. They will listen to my voice, and there will be one flock with one shepherd. The Father loves me because I sacrifice my life so I may take it back again. No one can take my life from me. I sacrifice it voluntarily. For I have the authority to lay it down when I want to and also to take it up again. For this is what my Father has commanded." (John 10:14-18)

Today, give thanks to Christ for how He held on to his life, then gave up His life to finally take it back up again. Remember, He sits at the right hand of the Father praying for you today, that you might live in the fullness of life that He died to win for you. Give thanks for the truth that the darkness can never extinguish Christ's light.

It is written: *"He entered the Most Holy Place once for all time and secured our redemption forever."* (Hebrews 9:12)

———•———

Let's pray...

Jesus, I thank you that your sacrifice was for me, and it was once and for all. I thank you that today I can live in your light, and in your presence, because the curtain is open forever. Amen.

DAY 38:
IT'S HIS SWORD, NOT YOURS!

———•———

"Get wisdom; develop good judgment. Don't forget my words or turn away from them."
(Proverbs 4:5)

As we learn to love the Word of God and how wield its truth in the face of the enemy, we will be able to journey through all kind of spiritual "terrain" and still be victorious. But before we celebrate the joys of being armed and dangerous, let's remind ourselves of some important truths.

Firstly, it's not our sword, it is His! Although we have as part of our spiritual armour *"the sword of the Spirit, which is the Word of God"* (Ephesians 6:17), we still trust in God as our ultimate fortress and protector:

"I do not trust in my bow; I do not count on my sword to save me. You are the one who gives us victory over our enemies; you disgrace those who hate us." (Psalm 44:6-7)

Secondly, just like Jesus was tempted, we will be tempted to lay the Word down and stop doing what it says. It's interesting that the enemy quoted Scripture left, right and centre, but of course he took it out of context and it held no power. We cannot simply speak out God's words and expect them to be effective if we are not putting them into action. We have to be rooted in relationship with God, with a desire to follow Him closely and obey Him wholeheartedly. Jesus spoke about those who would cry out, "Lord! Lord!" but who didn't really know Him. Consequently, they were not "known" by God.

"So why do you keep calling me 'Lord, Lord!' when you don't do what I say? I will show you what it's like when someone comes to me, listens to my teaching, and then follows it. It is like a person building a house who digs deep and lays the foundation on solid rock. When the floodwaters rise and break against that house, it stands firm because it is well built. But anyone who hears and doesn't obey is like a person who builds a house right on the ground, without a foundation. When the floods sweep down against that house, it will collapse into a heap of ruins." (Luke 6:46-49)

It is our obedience to what Jesus says that puts us on solid ground and leads us to be victorious.

The most powerful, victorious way to handle the word of God is to know it, think on it, speak it, and then also live it. The Psalmist writes of a victorious fruitful life saying,

"Oh, the joys of those who do not follow the advice of the wicked, or stand around with sinners, or join in with mockers. But they delight in the law of the Lord, meditating on it day and night. They are like trees planted along the riverbank, bearing fruit each season. Their leaves never wither, and they prosper in all they do. But not the wicked! They are like worthless chaff, scattered by the wind. They will be condemned at the time of judgment. Sinners will have no place among the godly. For the Lord watches over the path of the godly, but the path of the wicked leads to destruction." (Psalm 1:1-6)

The wonderful thing about a life with Jesus is that we are

living by grace, not by law, so we don't need to be legalistic in our relationship. However, just as most of us would put on clothes when we wake up, have breakfast, clean our teeth and do various other activities out of habit, so there are some spiritual habits which will prove their worth in your life. Meditating on the word is one such habit.

Let me pause and tell you about our family trips to the dentist. For us it's always a family outing, because if I don't book us all in, one of us (namely my husband) will end up forgetting and will go too long between check-ups! Normally, I love these visits. We have a great dentist and have been blessed to not need too many treatments. The visits are literally fun!

Now (don't tell my dentist this), on every visit my dentist would advise me to floss more regularly. I would agree, he would show me how, then I would go away and do it once or twice before forgetting for another six months. This was my usual pattern until recently.

I happened to strain the ligaments in my jaw (not from talking too much, in case you are wondering. I had fainted and fallen over). When my dentist appointment came round I still couldn't open my jaw very wide, or very comfortably, so to have an examination was, for the first time, very painful. The regular encouragement to floss and subsequent demonstration was additionally painful. I held it together whilst in the room, but as soon as I got out I burst into tears. I felt like my jaw would never recover. As a result of that pain – and the desire not to repeat it – I began a daily flossing routine to ensure that all future dental appointment were as short as possible. I had adopted a new activity which has now grown into a habit with benefits.

In the same way I want to encourage you to begin planning your next steps for a daily habit of meditating on the Word of God, so that you may continue to be equipped to be victorious. Start small with just a verse or two and establish a habit of meditating on those Bible verses, keeping them in mind throughout the day. Establish this as a habit.

It is written:

"It is not by force nor by strength, but by my Spirit, says the Lord of Heaven's Armies." (Zechariah 4:6)

———•———

Let's pray...

Father, I thank you for your Word. Thank you that I can grow in confidence daily by knowing and living by your Word. Thank you that it's never too late to start new habits and refresh old ones. Lord, please help me order my day so that I can continue mediating on your Word, that I might be victorious in all ways. Amen.

DAY 39:
JUST KEEP STARTING

———•———

"My child, listen to what I say, and treasure my commands."
(Proverbs 2:1)

A few years ago, whilst on holiday in America, our family was able to take in the sights and sounds of the Grand Canyon. Who knew that a hole in the ground could be so majestic! Gazing at the scenery I was moved to worship the Lord afresh. We decided to defy the standard tourist response of just standing at the top and marvelling, and ventured on a path down into the canyon. It was an hour's walk down the path into the canyon to see things from a different viewpoint.

We diligently read the tourist information which stressed the importance of taking necessary health and safety precautions: not walking in the heat of the midday sun, drinking only to quench thirst, and eating salty snacks were essential actions to apparently avoid death! We were intrepid as we set off on our excursion, back-packs loaded with water and salty snacks. The journey down for all five of us was lovely. Occasionally the screed was a little slippery, which added to the drama, but we made it to the viewing point in a reasonable time and enjoyed a rest with the most stunning view.

However, in the Canyon what goes down must come up and at some point we began our ascent. It was at this point that our then eleven year old daughter decided that it was too hard. I cannot begin to explain how traumatic her fussing became to us all. To begin with, we were all positive and encouraging, cheering her on. When that failed, our eldest daughter took to storytelling as a distraction, but that did not work either. In the end the family separated; Tim walking with the two happy children and me with the unhappy one.

What happened over the next hour was quite a profound spiritual moment for her and me as we battled the physical challenge. I simply wouldn't let her stop, because every time she paused it became more and more difficult for her to get going again. It was really becoming intolerable. In the heat, with exhaustion setting in, my daughter genuinely felt that she couldn't make it. However, leaving her in the Canyon was not an option! So I decided that rather than let her stop to have some rest I would just have to keep her going.

Every time she ground to a halt, complaining she couldn't make it and begging for a break, I put the palm of my hand (gently!) in the small of her back and allowed my walking momentum to kick-start hers. I said to her, "Just keep starting." She threatened to be sick or faint and I assured her that she could do both if she chose, but only when she reached the top. I had saved most of my water and so was drip feeding her from my supply as hers was long gone. Eventually, we made it to back to the top and caught up with the others. The success was overwhelming for my daughter and both of us learnt a lesson: however difficult the journey, you just need to "keep starting".

Every one of us have faced different battles at different times.

The enemy would like to fill our heads with the lie that we're not going to make it, we're not going to be victorious. But our loving Father wants to place His hand gently on our back and encourage us to keep starting. If we just keep starting the same thing, eventually we will finish.

Paul spoke of the significance of finishing what he had started when he addressed the Elders in Ephesus: *"But my life is worth nothing to me unless I use it for finishing the work assigned me by the Lord Jesus—the work of telling others the Good News about the wonderful grace of God"* (Acts 20:24). When he wrote to Timothy, Paul was glad to be able to write, *"I have fought the good fight, I have finished the race, and I have remained faithful"* (2 Timothy 4:7).

Paul encouraged Timothy to keep starting too, to persist in doing what God had called him to do. I encourage you to do the same!

"But don't let it faze you. Stick with what you learned and believed, sure of the integrity of your teachers—why, you took in the sacred Scriptures with your mother's milk! There's nothing like the written Word of God for showing you the way to salvation through faith in Christ Jesus. Every part of Scripture is God-breathed and useful one way or another—showing us truth, exposing our rebellion, correcting our mistakes, training us to live God's way. Through the Word we are put together and shaped up for the tasks God has for us." (2 Timothy 3:14-17 MSG)

As much as my daughter was fazed by the endurance required to complete the canyon climb, her tiredness was understandable. Jesus, in the wilderness, felt hungry and tired. Like Jesus, we can give thanks that we can lean on God, who never tires or grows weary and can sustain us through the most challenging times.

"The Lord is the everlasting God, the Creator of all the earth.

He never grows weak or weary. No one can measure the depths of his understanding. He gives power to the weak and strength to the powerless. Even youths will become weak and tired, and young men will fall in exhaustion. But those who trust in the Lord will find new strength. They will soar high on wings like eagles. They will run and not grow weary. They will walk and not faint." (Isaiah 40:28-31)

Today, even now, if you feel tired on your journey, remember that the Lord never tires. He will renew you. He will give you the strength you need.

It is written:

"So take a new grip with your tired hands and strengthen your weak knees. Mark out a straight path for your feet so that those who are weak and lame will not fall but become strong." (Hebrews 12:12-13)

————•————

Let's pray...

Father, I thank you that you are all I need to just keep starting. Today, I will just keep starting so that eventually I might finish what you have planned for me to do, for your glory. Amen.

DAY 40:
NO OPPORTUNITY

"A prudent person foresees danger and takes precautions. The simpleton goes blindly on and suffers the consequences."
(Proverbs 22:3)

At the end of forty days in the wilderness Luke tells us that, *"When the devil had finished tempting Jesus, he left him until the next opportunity came"* (Luke 4:13). The enemy is an opportunist who is looking to seize any opportunity we might give him. We therefore must remain guarded and vigilant with our eyes on the Lord. Don't give the enemy any opportunity! As Peter wrote,

"Stay alert! Watch out for your great enemy, the devil. He prowls around like a roaring lion, looking for someone to devour. Stand firm against him, and be strong in your faith. Remember that your family of believers all over the world is going through the same kind of suffering you are. In his kindness God called you to share in his eternal glory by means of Christ Jesus. So after you have suffered a little while, he will restore, support, and strengthen you, and he will place you on a firm foundation. All power to him forever!" (1 Peter 4:8-11)

Peter referred to the enemy as a roaring lion. This image is helpful in understanding one of the enemy's strategies. You may have been on a safari and seen lions hunt in the wild or seen it on TV. The key to success for most predators is in isolating a weak target. Lions seek to separate the young or the vulnerable from the herd, so that they are easier to take down. What is true in nature is true in the spiritual realm. If the enemy can isolate people then he can eventually wear them down.

For this reason we need to stay vigilant, stay connected. I am a local church girl in heart and actions. Time and again I've seen precious people isolate themselves from their church family and begin to drift in their faith and stop following Christ. It is possible to be in complete isolation and still follow the Lord, of course, but it is the exception to God's rule. He longs for the isolated to be in a family.

"God places the lonely in families; he sets the prisoners free and gives them joy." (Psalm 68:6)

The enemy will lead you to believe that you don't need the church and that the church doesn't need you. However, this is a strategy of destruction.

"Let us hold tightly without wavering to the hope we affirm, for God can be trusted to keep his promise. Let us think of ways to motivate one another to acts of love and good works. And let us not neglect our meeting together, as some people do, but encourage one another, especially now that the day of his return is drawing near." (Hebrews 10:23-25)

Let's encourage one another and look out for one another, like the workmen and soldiers who rebuilt the walls of Jerusalem with Nehemiah. Be armed and vigilant. Nehemiah ensured that all the workmen were also equipped with swords. He also positioned the people in such a way that they could defend each other.

"I placed armed guards behind the lowest parts of the wall in the

exposed areas. I stationed the people to stand guard by families, armed with swords, spears, and bows. Then as I looked over the situation, I called together the nobles and the rest of the people and said to them, 'Don't be afraid of the enemy! Remember the Lord, who is great and glorious, and fight for your brothers, your sons, your daughters, your wives, and your homes!'" (Nehemiah 4:13-14)

We are armed with the "sword of the Spirit, which is the Word of God" not just for our own benefit but for each other. We are called to be part of the body of Christ and fight for each other, young and old, male and female. It is time to be victorious and for this we need to sharpen our swords and join with the winning family.

The togetherness of believers is so important, which is why Paul encourages us to not to make a half-hearted effort but *"...every effort to keep yourselves united in the Spirit, binding yourselves together with peace. For there is one body and one Spirit, just as you have been called to one glorious hope for the future."* (Ephesians 4:3-4)

Clearly this task of being united in the Spirit is not a guaranteed "easy" task, otherwise Paul would not have warned us that it requires "every effort" to be made. But the promise of one glorious hope for the future should be incentive enough.

I've been privileged to serve alongside my husband in leading our church for nearly eighteen years. We are living in incredible days when the momentum of unity in the Church is gathering. The "gaps" between the members of our own church are diminishing as unity grows. Furthermore, significantly, the gaps between the churches across our town are diminishing too. Friendships are increasing. Differences are being put aside for the sake of the Gospel of Christ. But of course, this will unsettle the enemy of unity, the prince of division.

In so many ways I can liken it again to the work of Nehemiah. When his enemies *"heard that the work was going ahead and that the gaps in the wall of Jerusalem were being repaired they were furious. They all made plans to come and fight against Jerusalem and throw us into confusion. But we prayed to our God and guarded the city day and night to protect ourselves"* (Nehemiah 4:7-9)

Let us remain vigilant; let us stay connected; let us close the gaps between us and use our weapons against the enemy and not each other.

Today, as we come to the end of following Jesus through the wilderness, learning to become victorious in the battles we face, let us remember that it is in His strength and with His weapons that the victory comes. It is He who will equip us.

It is written:

"Now may the God of peace— who brought up from the dead our Lord Jesus, the great Shepherd of the sheep, and ratified an eternal covenant with his blood—may he equip you with all you need for doing his will. May he produce in you, through the power of Jesus Christ, every good thing that is pleasing to him. All glory to him forever and ever! Amen." (Hebrews 13:20-21)

———•———

Let's pray...

Lord, thank you for your victory on the cross that enables me to know victory in any battle that I might face. Thank you that you will equip me with everything I need for being victorious in you, for your glory. May your will be done in and through me. Amen.

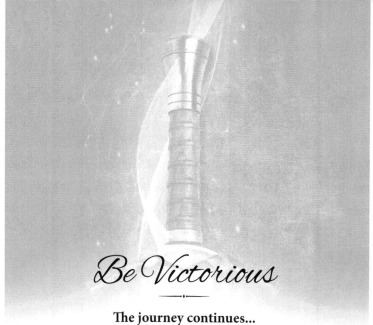

Be Victorious

The journey continues...

We have come to the end of our journey through the wilderness with Jesus, but for each of us the journey continues. We will continue to face the same temptations as He did – to lay aside His identity; to doubt God's ability to provide for us and meet all our needs; to try to make His purposes happen in our lives through our own strength, instead of relying on His...

The good news is that Jesus continues to journey with us. We are never alone. Keep your eyes fixed on Jesus. Instead of becoming worried or anxious, turn your anxiety into prayer. Determine to keep trusting in God's goodness and love towards you, despite your current circumstances. Above all, get to know your sword really well and practice wielding it, often! Then, no matter what troubles or attacks may come, you will be able to walk victorious.

About the Author

Helen is the Executive Minister of Wellspring Church, a multi-ethnic, multi-congregational church family based in Watford, just outside London. She and her husband have lived in the Watford area since the mid-1990s and have been leading Wellspring Church together since 1998.

Drawing from a range of experience in the hotel business, overseas mission, Christian youth work and raising three enthusiastic children, Helen has become a strategic leader and an inspiring communicator who loves connecting people to the liberating truth of God's word. She enjoys time with her family, good books, regular exercise and holidays.

Follow her on Twitter: @HelenRoberts_1